YOUR KNOWLEDGE H

- We will publish your bachelor's and master's thesis, essays and papers

- Your own eBook and book - sold worldwide in all relevant shops

- Earn money with each sale

Upload your text at www.GRIN.com and publish for free

Bibliographic information published by the German National Library:

The German National Library lists this publication in the National Bibliography; detailed bibliographic data are available on the Internet at http://dnb.dnb.de .

Imprint:

Copyright © 2014 GRIN Verlag
Print and binding: Books on Demand GmbH, Norderstedt Germany
ISBN: 9783668646858

This book at GRIN:

https://www.grin.com/document/413445

Fuad Babayev

The Export Competition between Germany and China

GRIN Verlag

GRIN - Your knowledge has value

Since its foundation in 1998, GRIN has specialized in publishing academic texts by students, college teachers and other academics as e-book and printed book. The website www.grin.com is an ideal platform for presenting term papers, final papers, scientific essays, dissertations and specialist books.

Visit us on the internet:

http://www.grin.com/

http://www.facebook.com/grincom

http://www.twitter.com/grin_com

MASTER THESIS

EXPORT COMPETITION BETWEEN GERMANY AND CHINA

Presented by

Fuad Babayev

University of Flensburg

European Studies

University of Flensburg

International Institute for Management

Professorship for International Economy

18 March 2014

ABSTRACT

This master thesis researches the export competition between Germany and China. Russian market has been selected as an example in order to explain ongoing export competition in facts and figures. It has been noted that, competition is not only about battle of winners and losers, but it is also about impact of competition on growth and innovation of the economies. Following, the thesis finds out how competition impacts the growth and innovation of their economy and what further actions could be taken in this regard.

The ideas regarding the impact of competition on growth and modernization are controversial in economic literature and therefore different concepts are analysed. Moreover, the competitiveness of export masters has been researched which is an important part of international trade. The competitiveness of China and Germany is considered according to several criteria, which will be mentioned later in the thesis.

Germany and China play a significant role in the world trade and they have bigger shares in imports of different states. These countries have various export strategies in the world trade and in spite of this fact both of them could be considered successful in terms of international trade. Russia is in the list of 20 biggest importers of the world where the share of imports from China and Germany comprise substantial part.

It is notable to stress the fact that since 2010 China has won leadership in Russian market over Germany who has been a number first exporter for a long time. The sales of China to Russia has ever since further increased and exceeded the volume of German exports. This ongoing competition process and its analysis through competition theory take core place in the thesis.

I

TABLE OF CONTENTS

LIST OF FIGURES

IV

LIST OF TABLES

LIST OF ABBREVIATIONS

AHK – *Ausenhandelskammer*

CEE - Central and Eastern European

CompNet - Competitiveness Research Network

DIHK – Deutscher Industrie und Handelskammertag

FIE – Foreign Invested Enterprise

FRG - Federal Republic of Germany

FTC – Foreign Trade Company

GCI – Global Competitiveness Index

GCR – Global Competitiveness Report

GDR - German Democratic Republic

GTAI – German Trade and Invest

LSE - London School of Economics

MEDR – Ministry of Economic Development of Russia

MMC - Monopolies and Mergers Commission

OA – *Ost-Aussschuss*

PISA – Program for International Student Assessment

PNE – Production Network for Exports

PPP – Purchasing Power Parity

RCEP - Research Centre for Economic Performance

SEZ – Special Economic Zone

SME – Small and Medium size Enterprise

TFP – Total Factor Productivity

1 INTRODUCTION

The international trade has been exposed to significant changes especially because of globalization process. The countries are opening borders, removing barriers for trade and adopting proper trade policies. In terms of trade, globalization offers both opportunities for countries and competition pressure. (Gorodnichenko et al, 2008, p. 3) The rapid growth of Chinese exports has put many world countries including EU under tough competition pressure. It has caused concerns and raised the question about competitiveness of European countries against China. (Bekovskis et al, 2014, p. 1)

As the biggest economy and exporter of Europe Germany also encounters challenges from China. The focus of this thesis is to research the impacts of export competition between Germany and China. In order to have a deep look into the topic, the export competition of the countries on the Russian market has also been researched. Russia has been selected because it is bigger trade partner of both countries. The motivation to write this thesis has been to research the fact that since 2010 China has won leadership in Russian market where Germany has for a long time been number first exporter. (Internet Portal of Foreign Trade, MEDR, 2013) This fact encouraged investigating the factors that make Chinese and German exports successful and impacts of export competition on their economy. Several theories and concepts explain positive and negative impact of competition. These theories have been applied in the thesis.

Obstacles to competition emerging because of improper government policies or anti-competitive practice by companies are wide-spread in developing countries. Such kind of situation limits the possibilities for innovation and growth; deteriorates the condition of buyers. Oppositely, competitive market enables to invest effectively on different spheres of economy, including education, R&D and infrastructure.

The impact of competition on growth has not been commonly agreed by researchers and there exist controversial ideas. According to Aghion (2002) there is an inverted U relationship between competition and innovation where market rewards the innovators.

1

He has later reconciled this theory with Schumpeterian model allowing incumbent firms to innovate that are near to technological frontier. (Aghion et al, 2002, p. 3) Inverted U relationship is effective when the initial level of competition is little so that the laggards have a chance to benefit and survive. (Aghion et al, 2002, p. 4)

The main opponent of this theory is Schumpeterian concept, which presumes that competition reduces the growth and innovation because the scope of the reward to innovators is limited because of tough competition. (Onori, 2013, p. 3) According to Schumpeter the competitive markets are not the most effective institutions to encourage innovation and growth. The stimulus to innovate is the distinction between the profits that can be obtained with investment on research and development or without it. (Gilbert, 2006, p. 159)

According to GCR 2013/2014 the competitiveness of a country is a set of institutions and factors that determine the level of productivity. It determines 12 pillars of competitiveness that have been covered in the next chapters. (GCR, 2013/2014, p. 4)

Atkinson (2013) supports the idea that competitiveness is related to economic health of region's or nation's traded sectors. Under the term economic health the scientist means several factors like jobs and value added. (The amount of value that traded sector firms add to the inputs of production that they purchase). According to author the true definition of competitiveness is capacity of the region to export in more value added terms than it imports. (Atkinson, 2013, p. 2) Moreover, the author states that artificial measures applied by government like discounts, artificial low taxes and currency, subsidies and barriers on imports don't contribute to competitiveness. Such policies may increase the trade surplus but they will not make a nation competitive. In contrast the competitive nation is the one that has trade surplus, few obstacles on imports and limited discounts for exporters. (Atkinson, 2013, p. 3)

The competitiveness of markets is not automatically created business climate but rather is a result of appropriate government policy. There should

2

be no irrelevant obstacles hindering the entry of the company to the market and at the same time the massive exit of the companies because of certain reasons should be regulated by the government. (Godfrey, 2008, p. 4) There is a linkage between domestic and international competitiveness. If the companies of the country are not competitive in internal market then these firms have few chances to win competition in international trade. (Godfrey, 2008, p. 5)

There is observed tough competition between German and Chinese companies over the Russian market. Russia is among 20 biggest importers and it is largest country of the world. The country is rich with resources and it acts as an important supplier of energy resources for both Germany and China. In spite of the fact that, traditionally Germany has been export leader in Russian market in the last few years China has gained the leadership position. The exports of China to Russia have grown very rapidly in a short period of time. The reason of this shift in export leadership has been studied in the thesis.

There are many German and Chinese companies operating in Russia and the competition between them is very intense. This rivalry pushes both sides for innovation of their technologies and get more shares in world markets. From the perspective of competition and innovation theory this ongoing process has a positive impact on innovation and growth of economies.

The impact of Chinese exports on Germany is ambivalent. On the one hand it strengthens the purchase capacity of consumers and Chinese cheaper input products used for production make Germany competitive in the world markets. On the other hand the export destinations of China and Germany overlap in many world markets including in Russia and it overheats the competition.

The studies of Bekovskis and Silgoner (2013) have shown that Germany is less exposed to crowding out pressure of China and it is competitive to withstand competition. Mostly small and peripheral European countries have encountered tough crowding out from China. (Bekovskis & Silgoner, 2013, p. 7)

3

Moreover, the competition pressure affects positively on skill upgrading of European countries. In the case of Belgium, statistics show that competition pressure from China accounted for 42% skill improvement in Belgian firms. (Mion and Zhu, p. 2)

The competition pressure from China pushes European companies for technological upgrading and between 2000 and 2007 it accounted for 15% technological development. In the same period the patents per worker has increased simultaneously. (Bloom, Draca & Van Reenen, 2011, p. 4)

However, the conducted survey among German companies, politicians and various groups show that the opinions are contradictory. 80% of surveyed economic decision-makers and 70% of German politicians perceive China as a threat rather than enrichment for economy. (Huawei Studies & Infratest research institute, 2012, p 88) Especially the companies are worried about price policy of China, which puts German companies under hard situation. (Huawei Studies & Infratest research institute, 2012, p 90) The economic decision-makers are mainly concerned about three important branches like automobile industry, machinery and Information technologies. (Huawei Studies & Infratest research institute, 2012, p. 94) The exports of China to Germany for 2011 have been 79.3 billion Euros and vice versa 64.8 billion Euros. (Huawei Studies & Infratest research institute, 2012, p 26)

The number of German companies in China and oppositely increase periodically from which both sides benefit. Germany takes advantage from enormous internal market of China and at the same time huge labour force and China benefits from technological transfer from German side. (Huawei Studies & Infratest research institute, 2012, p. 98)

The growing environmental problems in the world necessitate switching to green technologies and renewable energies. These new areas of industry are also becoming subject to competition that requires from both sides the best green technology innovations.

It can decrease the dependence of both countries from natural resources and make them even more competitive in the world markets. This issue is discussed in the last chapter of the thesis.

Is China a threat for Germany or enrichment for its economy? Does competition really cause the growth and innovation of German and Chinese economies? These questions will be answered in the next chapters.

2 HYPOTHESIS FORMATION

The core point of this thesis will be to research the impact of export competition on growth and innovation of German and Chinese economies. In this respect competition and innovation theory, competitiveness and Schumpeterian concept will be explored.

- Competition, growth and innovation– According to Aghion (2002) there is an inverted U relationship between competition and innovation. They are correlative.
- Schumpeterian theory seeks to state that competition is not the best way to increase the economy and it reduces the rewards for innovators.
- Competitiveness includes many factors that make a nation competitive in the world markets.

Traditional industrial organization theories have supported the idea that, the product market competition lowers the innovation because the scope of reward is reduced with high number of competitors. In contrast if there is a monopoly then the reward for an innovator is big and it stimulates the monopolist to innovate.

However, recent studies by Aghion (2002) and other scientists have showed a positive relationship between product market competition and innovation. These empirical researches have also reconciled the Schumpeterian paradigm and formed new approaches. (Aghion et al, 2002, p. 2) Accordingly, the incumbent firms whose technological opportunities are near to frontier they will resist new entries and innovate furthermore. If the company is far from technological frontier then in case of entry they will be driven out. (Aghion et al, 2002, p. 3)

5

Schumpeterian theory claims that the stimulus to innovate is the financial interest of the company how much capital is it going to make out of new innovation. Provided that the profit from innovation will be high the company will invest into innovation, in contrast when there is tough competition the incentive for innovation will be reduced. Schumpeter stressed the importance of intellectual property rights so the innovator enjoys its invention fully. (Gilbert, 2006, p. 159)

Competitiveness is a broad term that has been a topic for intensive debates among scientists. The pillars of competitiveness that have been reflected in GCI 2013/2014 are applied on our respected countries in order to measure their competitiveness. Moreover, the future perspectives and sustainability of German and Chinese exports have been considered.

In order to make rational outcome for the thesis and relate above-mentioned theories to our case three concepts will be important. Firstly, the theory of authors who support the positive correlation between innovation and competition will be considered. Secondly, Schumpeterian effect will be applied to look at different models of the impact of competition on growth and innovation. Thirdly, the pillars of competitiveness will be employed to research the competitiveness of China and Germany.

Thus, the thesis will focus on the impact of export competition on growth and innovation of German and Chinese economies. Following it will seek to answer these questions:

Does the export competition between China and Germany contribute to the growth and innovation of their economies?

As it was mentioned above, according to the theory of Aghion (2002) there is an inverted U relationship between competition and growth. The companies of each country can be successful if they invest into R&D and make innovations. There is also Schumpeterian effect determining competition as a negative factor for innovation. The competition pressure from China has caused for growth of patents in Europe. In the next chapters of the thesis this fact will be explained through scientific researches.

Consequently there is a framework for both sides to innovate and increase economic growth.

Are both economies enough competitive in order to co-exist?

In order to understand this question the competitiveness of both sides will be investigated. Chinese and German firms are considered to be proportionally competitive and there are evidences that competition does not result with massive exits of any side.

Is China a threat for German exports?

To answer this question the survey conducted by TNS Infratest among German companies, politicians, social groups and statistical data regarding export volumes of Germany to Russia in different periods will be explored.

2.1 METHODOLOGY

This thesis heavily founds on several economic theories that mainly are related to competition and innovation. Different economical articles have been intensively used to look deeper into the topic. The author seeks to explore the theories of competition and then check their impact on economies of China and Germany. In order to implement it several theories will be applied: competition theory, Schumpeterian concept, competitiveness and different attitudes to these theories.

There exist different school of thought and their view on the impact of competition on innovation and growth is contradictory. Thus the author will consider all theories and focus mainly on the concepts on which the theorists have reconciled their ideas.

The statistical data regarding GDP, FDI, export volume in different periods, economic growth rate, surveys and etc will be highlighted. These data will be described also in the form of diagrams. Case studies have been also used in the thesis in order to provide examples regarding the impact of competition on increase and modernization. There have been used various sources in three languages: German, English and Russian.

Finally the main method of this paper is to build theoretical foundation and then apply it to the practice.

2.2 DESIGN OF THE THESIS

The beginning of the thesis includes theoretical foundation regarding competitiveness, competition, innovation and growth. It will lead to the empirical considerations and research to be made.

The empirical share of the thesis will highlight the conducted researches and evidences in the specific area of economics to discuss the issues of competition, innovation, growth and competitiveness.

Consequently, the empirical research will contribute to answering main question of the thesis.

3 LITERATURE VIEW

3.1 THEORETICAL FOUNDATION

The core point of the thesis is competition and first this concept should be clarified. In general competition is the rivalry between entities (countries, companies and etc.) who strive for gaining maximum profit. (Godfrey, 2008, p. 3)

There are classified two types of competition: perfect and imperfect competition. Imperfect competition exists when there are few sellers who are dominating the market. It has several forms like monopoly, oligopoly, and etc. (Policonomics economic dictionary, 2012)

Perfect competition defines the market that the members are not enough powerful to control the market and fix the price. Perfect competition rarely exists in world markets but its efficiency is different according to countries. There are several features of perfect competition:

- No obstacles for entry and exit
- Awareness of participants
- Property rights

8

- Awareness of participants
- Homogenous products
- Unlimited number of sellers, consumers, and etc.

This type of competition will not fully exist if above mentioned criteria are not met. The market has to be free for all participants so they trade equally. Moreover, the awareness of consumers regarding the products enables them to make rational choice and to be well informed about price, quality, product description and etc. The competition cannot exist without proper policy and therefore effective functioning of institutions or agencies are needed. (Policonomics economic dictionary, 2012) So far we explained the core point of the competition and in the next chapters the impact of competition on growth and innovation will be highlighted.

3.2 COMPETITION AND INNOVATION

As it was mentioned in previous chapters there is still not common point on the relationship between competition and innovation. Schumpeterian concept believes that there is a negative correlation between competition and innovation, because the competition reduces the rents from which the monopoly profits. Aghion (2002) and other scientists have noted to positive relationship between competition and innovation.

However, they have modified Schumpeterian model by allowing incumbent firms to innovate. The companies who are near to technological frontier are forced to innovate in order to escape competition because competition decreases their pre innovation rents. The figure 1 describes how competition affects both advanced and laggard firms.

Figure 1 – Impact of competition on TFP growth in technologically advanced and laggard firms

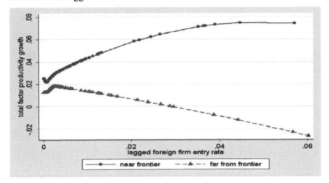

Source: OECD (2008, p.19)

By innovating technological leaders will increase post innovation rents to some extent. The firms who are away from technological border will have no incentive to innovate because first they have to reach the level of market leaders and then innovate in order to progress.

Therefore intensive competition will negatively affect laggard companies and reduce their post innovation rents. Shortly said when the level of competition is low there is a chance for laggards to take profit, but in the case of intense competition only neck and neck companies will be able to survive and escape competition by innovating. Neck and neck firms are those who have lower unit costs and they are considered leaders of the market. (Aghion et al, 2001, p. 4)

Aghion (2001) and the co-authors have brought the activity of UK companies as an evidence of positive correlation between competition and innovation. The empirical research is founded on several UK firms including the period of 1968-1997. (Aghion et al, 2001, p. 5) This period is convenient to study the impact of competition on innovation because at this time lots of changes and reforms took place. These changes were due to execution of EU Single Market program, reforms after the investigation of MMC under the Fair Trading Act and huge privatizations. (Aghion et al, 2001, p. 25)

10

The data includes 461 companies and out of them 236 are with patent. The data from US patent Office has been extensively used in the studies. (Aghion et al, 2001, p. 26) The conducted research has measured innovative product, the level of competition in the industry, the degree of technological gap between companies (neck and neckness) and threat of bankruptcy. (Aghion et al, 2001, p. 27)

Aghion (2001) also claims that when there is a financial pressure on the firm and it is near to fall into debts the chance for innovation is higher. Because the firm will have to innovate in order to reduce the costs and avoid bankruptcy. (Aghion et al, 2001, 44) The conducted research established the following:

- There is an inverted U relationship between competition and innovation
- The equilibrium level of technological "neck and neckness" among firms decrease with competition
- The higher the "neck and neckness" in an industry, the deeper U relationship between competition and innovation (Aghion et al, 2001, p. 43)

The equilibrium level of technological neck and neckness among companies diminishes with competition and the larger the level of neck and neckness in the market, the deeper is the inverted U relationship between competition and innovation. Schumpeterian theory dominates when the degree of competition is high and laggards cannot catch up with innovators. Another point that Aghion (2001) and his colleagues put forward is debt pressure which makes firms innovate especially in the low levels of competition. The usage of empirical researches and evidence regarding UK firms confirm inverted U relationship between competition and innovation. (Aghion et al, 2001, p. 45)

Gilbert (2006) has researched competition and innovation focusing mainly on intellectual property rights that have a big impact on research and development. R&D is a driving engine that stays behind the innovation. (Gilbert, 2006, p. 160)

The author states that exclusive rights create stimulus for modernization in high competitive markets and nonexclusive rights have opposite effect. (Gilbert, 2006, p. 192)

However, there are some exceptions, which will be discussed in the thesis. The power of intellectual property protection is a big factor for profit from invention because it defines to what extent the owner can enjoy the new invention. If the inventor has an opportunity to license new discovery then the amount of profit will be high. (Gilbert, 2006, p. 162) In contrast if an inventor does not have strength to prevent the invention from imitation the profitability will decrease. In general the new inventions are protected according to exclusive intellectual property rights like patent. By using patent the inventor will be able to maximize the profit and to raise the value of discovery. However, the patent will not stop the competition from other firms who can discover something around of new invention. (Gilbert, 2006, p. 163)

Competition affects negatively on R&D if there exist nonexclusive rights as there is no protection for inventors. (Gilbert, 2006, p. 204) However, it is unrealistic to believe that most markets grant such rights for inventers and therefore most of them prefer to keep the discovery in secrecy. If compare the monopolist who has full intellectual property right and the firm in competitive market, then the latter has more incentive for modernization. The monopolist enjoys the benefits from old technology and it has less incentive to innovate as the profits from old technology will be lost. There is not pressure on the monopolist from other firms. Arrow shows that, the company with exclusive rights in competitive market will have more stimuli for innovation. (Gilbert, 2006, p. 165)

Gorodnichenko (2008) and other scientists focus mainly on the impact of globalization on innovation in their studies. According to authors large multinational companies and their supply chain all over the world contribute to the transfer of knowledge and other capabilities to domestic firms. Apart from it the external competition also drives domestic firms to innovate and withstand the rivalry. The authors claim that innovation by domestic firms takes place mainly because of foreign direct investment and foreign competition. (Gorodnichenko et al, 2008, p. 31)

These above mentioned concepts and theories will be researched in the case of China and Germany.

3.3 COMPETITION AND GROWTH

So far we discussed several theories regarding the relationship between competition and modernization. There is also a linkage between innovation and growth. The first creates better technologies, which affect directly the growth. (OECD, 2007, p. 6)   Godfrey as many other authors supported the idea that there is a positive correlation between competition and growth. Competition enables the firms to make manufacture and allocation efficient, to apply advanced machinery and to modernize. These determinants of productivity contribute to growth. (Godfrey, 2008, p. 11) Onori (2013) gives a different interpretation to the relationship between competition and growth. The author shows spill over effect as the main driving engine behind the growth. (Onori, 2013, p. 3) The model offered by Onori distinguishes intra-sectoral spill over and points to positive impact of technology transfer on growth. (Onori, 2013, p. 7)

Aghion and Bessonova used the data of Russian companies as evidence to the positive relationship between competition and growth. In the previous chapter we also mentioned the data panel of British companies regarding the correlation between competition and innovation. The data of Russian companies have been taken from different state committees and institutions. The research has shown positive impact of foreign entry on Russian local market. The data covers around 15 000 firms that functioned during 1996-2002 years. It also includes 70% of industrial output and employment in Russia. (Aghion & Bessonova, 2006, p. 269) The studies of authors have pointed to Schumpeterian effect regarding the capability of less efficient firms for competition. The laggard companies of Russia have not been effective in competition against foreign entrants. (Aghion & Bessonova, 2006, p. 271) Moreover the foreign competitors have demonstrated higher productivity and employment than domestic firms. The foreign entry has also encouraged the firms near to technological frontier to innovate and grow furthermore. (Aghion & Bessonova, 2006, p. 270)

13

3.4   COMPETITIVENESS

The term competitiveness has also caused to debates and discussions in order to give the correct explanation. The scientist of Harvard Business School Michael Porter and Global Competitiveness Index connect this term to productivity of the country. Atkinson gives a different point of view regarding competitiveness assuming that it should not be equated to productivity or GDP growth.

According to the author the competitiveness is the capability of the region to export more in value added terms than importing them. (Atkinson, 2013, p. 2) The trade policies of government employed in the framework of competitiveness like discounts, artificial low currency, and reduced wages in export sectors, artificial low taxes, subsidies and barriers on imports are considered factors not enhancing competitiveness. In spite of the fact that, in 1980s USA managed to limit trade deficit with lower currency value the competitiveness of the country remained unchanged. Finally the author states that the competitive economy is the one, which has trade surplus, few obstacles to imports and less discount for exporters. (Atkinson, 2013, p. 3)

The World Economic Forum in its global competitiveness report (2013-2014) covered the growth rate in 148 countries. (GCR, 2013/2014, p. 13) The report distinguishes 12 pillars in order to find out determinants of competitiveness and productivity. As we see from the figure 2 the first pillar is institutions that play very important role in creation of legal and administrative framework where the firms interact in order to gain profit. The importance of public institutions has been noted in economic literature as they have main power in allocation of resources and management of finances. (GCR, 2013/2014, p. 4)

The efficient infrastructure is needed in order to provide the companies with better facilities for their activity. Communication and transport infrastructure play a key role in connecting the regions and as a result less developed areas get access to economic centres. (GCR, 2013/2014, p. 5) If a country strives for production of value added goods it should consider improving its education system.

14

Qualitative education can provide firms with high skilled labour force that stays behind production of high technologies. (GCR, 2013/2014, p. 6) Technological readiness is one of the factors that a country needs to have in order to produce at lower costs and with high quality.

FDI can be a contribution for economies of less developed countries in terms of technology. (GCR, 2013/2014, p. 8) Another determinant of competitiveness is regarded market size. The bigger market size enables to benefit from economies of scale. Economies of scale imply that when the firm expands and the amount of output increases the costs of production lowers. Al Marshall differentiates internal and external economies of scale. When a firm decreases the costs and raises production then internal economies of scale have been accomplished. External economies of scale take effect when there is a better infrastructure and a firm benefiting from it can transport products easily to a bigger area. (Hekal, 2009) In the next chapters we will discuss how economies of scale function in Germany and China.

Figure 2 - GCI 12 pillars of competitiveness

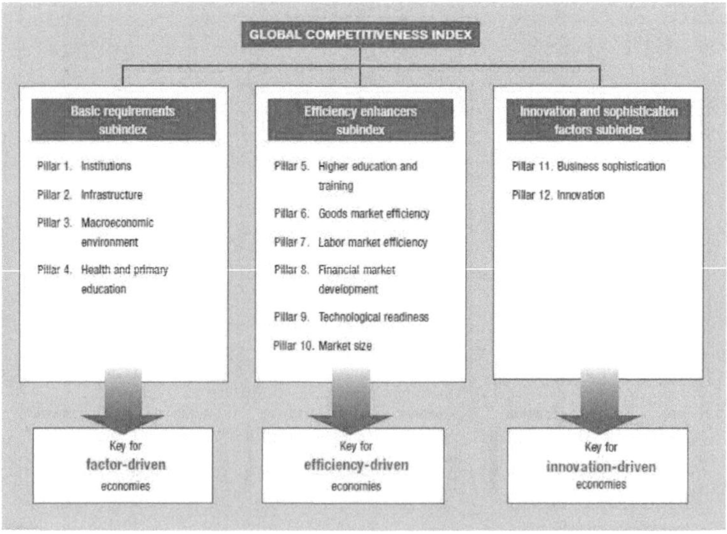

Source: GCR (2013/2014, p. 9)

15

So far the determinants of competitiveness were discussed that eventually lead to growth of the economy. These pillars of competitiveness are interdependent and alone they will not be effective. For example it seems impossible to foster innovation of the technology without well education that prepare highly skilled labour force. Alternatively, in other case, the improper policies of public institutions might destroy the business atmosphere of the country. Later these determinants will be used to analyse the competitiveness of Germany and China in Russian market.

4 GERMAN AND CHINESE EXPORT ECONOMY

Exports comprise an essential part of German and Chinese economies. In this section the composition, trade partners, sustainability and strategy of their exports will be researched. Germany has started to reform and rebuild its economy after the Second World War and since then it has succeeded to be a welfare country. Starting from 50s German foreign trade grows in a positive direction. The figure 3 is describing increasing tempo of German foreign trade starting from the year of 2000.

Figure 3 – Growth rate of German foreign trade

Development of German foreign trade

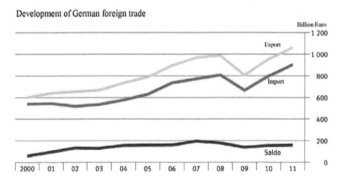

Source: *Statistische Bundesamt* (2011, p. 6)

Since year of 2000 the exports of Germany have grown 77% and imports 68%. The trade balance saldo has even 167% risen. (Destatis, 2011, p. 7)

16

The main importing countries of German products are EU member states, Russia, Turkey, USA and China. (Destatis, 2011, p. 8) Germany has concentrated on production of value added products like automobile, machinery, data processing equipment, chemical products and others. Last 10 years these four spheres have made up 45-48% of all exports. The industry sectors like paper and cardboard, furniture, textile that were 15 years ago export capable, now have lost export value. The main reason for removal of these areas is tough competition with Asian countries. In contrast the areas like pharmacy has grown up to 40 million Euros. (Yalchin & Zacher, 2011, p. 22)

Figure 4 - The share of certain products in German exports

Export according to important product groups 2011
in %

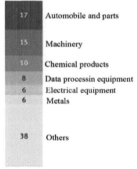

Source: Destatis (2011, p. 14)

As it was mentioned in previous chapters many job places in Germany are dependent on exports of the country. 39.1 million Employees in the year of 2000 were dependent on exports and this number rose up to 40.5 million in 2010. (Yalchin & Zacher, 2011, p. 23)

The main export countries of Germany are located in Europe and 71% of all German exports fall into their share. (Destatis, 2011, p. 10) Currently the biggest trade partner of Germany in Europe is France whose import share from Germany makes up around 90 billion Euros.

17

Out of Europe US also is one of the biggest export destinations for Germany and in 2010, the export volume to this country comprised 65 billion Euros. (Yalchin & Zacher, 2011, p. 19) The share of Russia, Turkey and Switzerland also increases rapidly. (Yalchin & Zacher, 2011, p. 20) The figure 5 is describing shares of European countries in the exports of Germany.

Figure 5 - Export destinations of Germany

Share of European countries in the exports of Germany

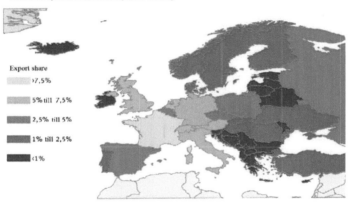

Export share
>7,5%
5% till 7,5%
2,5% till 5%
1% till 2,5%
<1%

Source: Destatis (2011, p. 10)

The main trading partners in Asia are China, India, Japan and South Korea. The exports to BRIC countries grow periodically and make them very important export destination land for Germany. The share of BRIC countries in German exports has grown from 1% in the year of 1990 up to 10% in the year of 2010. Since the year of 2000 the volume of exports to China and Russia has five times increased. In 2008 China and Russia shared more than 3% of all German exports and in 2009 despite the financial crisis in the world the share of China increased up to 4.5%. (Yalchin/ Zacher, 2011, p. 20) Periodically the importance of China for Germany rises and many German companies establish their subsidiaries in this country and profit from the huge local market and rich labour force.

The USA is not already the biggest trade partner of Germany and this place is taken by China. The figure 6 shows the development rate of trade with the USA and China.

Figure 6: German trade with the USA and China

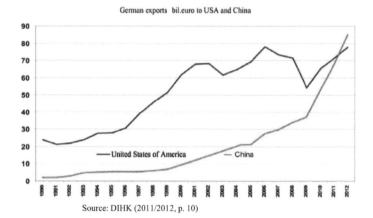

German exports bil.euro to USA and China

Source: DIHK (2011/2012, p. 10)

So far we discussed the export volume of Germany with different countries, the figures and exported main products. There emerges a logical question: what makes German exports successful? There are many hypotheses regarding the development of German exports but 4 main factors will be discussed in the thesis:

- Better cost competitiveness
- Cooperation with emerging markets
- Growing demand for technology
- Relocation of production (Danninger & Joutz, 2007, p. 3)

Starting from 1990s Germany encountered several difficult situations that had a negative impact on its economy and on its overall export: The reunification of Germany in 1990, the entrance of cheap labour force rich Asian countries into world market, European economic integration and etc. (Danninger & Joutz, 2007, p. 4)

After reunification Germany has had to spend much on developing eastern part of the country and to reduce wage gap between regions. On the one hand the wages in the newly joined eastern part had to be raised; on the other hand competitiveness had to be kept in order to be successful in the world trade. Fortunately, Germany managed to keep balance between salary increase and productivity. Every year the wage growth remained behind the productivity level. Average wage increase since 2003 fluctuated between 1-2% and this enabled German industry to keep competitiveness. Some authors argue that, cost competitiveness contributed to export growth and even normal wage could have increased domestic demand. (Danninger & Joutz, 2007, p. 5)

Germany has been successful in establishing mutually beneficial trade relationships with growing Asian markets. Fast growing Asian countries need technologies in order to transform their industry and increase productivity. Germany has been able to specialize on certain areas of industry and produce high quality technologies. This effective specialization enabled the country to provide booming economies with needed products. In this regard China plays very important role. The exports of Germany to this country have increased many times since the year of 2000 and German companies have been able to get share in Chinese market. Apart from it the trade with India and South Korea has grown considerably.

Germany is regarded to be the biggest trade partner of China in Europe and moreover it has biggest market share in Asia among all of EU countries. Another aspect that has fostered German exports is regarded to be relocation of its production facilities across the world. This enabled German firms to enjoy from lower production costs for intensive production processes. The larger companies established subsidiaries in different countries and goods exchange between them increased enormously. (Danninger & Joutz, 2007, p. 6) The figure 7 describes the impact of outsourcing and off-shoring.

Figure 7

Wage Costs for German Companies from Outsourcing and Off-Shoring

Unit Labor Cost Relative to Germany

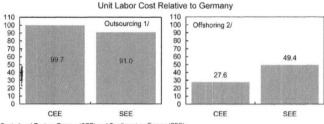

Central and Eastern Europe (CEE) and Southeastern Europe (SEE).

Source: IMF (2007, p. 31)

So far we mentioned several factors that make Germany successful, but there could be taken some steps to keep sustainability and growth. Raising internal demand should be focused on improving conditions for investment and innovation in the domestic market. For this purpose some tough regulations in the sphere of services should be mitigated and innovation with financial investments on research and development should be supported. Another important aspect is labour market of Germany that has confronted with shortage of highly skilled workers. Some experts regard that, involving older generation for working and females for full time jobs, removing barriers for highly skilled migrants, reforming education can contribute to the efficiency of labour market. (OECD, 2012, p. 3)

GCR (2013/2014) also shows the biggest problems of Germany as tax and restrictive labour regulations, tax rates and etc. Measures regarding environment protection also take core place in the future development of German economy and overall exports. The production is accustomed to the requirements of environmental protection and the country aims to benefit more from renewable energy sources. However, CO_2 level is still relatively high in spite of the fact that, country puts efforts to prevent it. (OECD, 2012, p. 21)

China has started to reform its economy since 1978 and opened its doors to world market. (Tsen, 2006, p. 2) This contributed to the growth of economy and the growth rate in 1979 was 6.1%, whereas this number rose up to 8.2% in the period of 1980-1999.

21

In 2002 the growth rate lagged behind the previous levels and made up 7.3%. The export growth rate was changing periodically from 1980 till 2002. (Tsen, 2006, p. 5)

The entrance of the country to the World trade organization led to structural changes and reforms of the economy. Moreover, the membership enabled China to integrate into the world economy and strengthen its share in the international markets. Before accession to WTO China had already started to remove barriers to trade, increase private sector by privatisations of state owned industries and creating health business atmosphere for foreign investors. (OECD, 2012, p. 50) In addition membership to WTO accelerated this process and China continued to reform its regulations especially in the area of agriculture, services and removed many tariffs hindering the development of trade. The peak of the reforms was adoption of anti-monopoly law in 2008 which substituted the previous competition law that was not enough functional. The new law strengthened the competition atmosphere in the local market and raised competitiveness of domestic firms in the international markets. (OECD, 2012, p. 53)

Preparation and execution of export strategy led China to success and this strategy was carried out with effective local policies. The creation of special economic zones is a part of this strategy and this policy involved establishment of zones and open cities where trade, financial operations, production, banking and different business activities occurred in a free environment in compare of other parts of the country. These zones served as attractive business area for both local and foreign investors among who mainly active were Hong-Kong and Taiwanese investors. SEZs played a key role in transforming the cities where they were established into huge business centres. Two of them Guangdong and Fujian have become bigger cities attracting many investors around the world. (Panagariya, 2003, p. 2)

SEZs offered many possibilities for entrepreneurs that made them attractive. The corporate income tax is 33% for foreign owned company and 55% for state owned firms, but in SEZs this figure is 15%. Moreover, the facilities employed for exports or sold inside of the SEZs are exempted of duties and taxes.

The companies are provided with tax holidays up to 5 years relying upon amount of the investment, period of the project, used technology and etc. The SEZs showed extraordinary results and more than half of investments and total exports came to their share. (Panagariya, 2003, p. 3)

In the past China has been known as a country exporting mainly labour-intensive products like textile, however sectoral targeting changed this direction and diversified manufacture of the companies. For this purpose production networks for exports (PNEs) were established and higher exchange retention rights were given to targeted sectors.

The creation purpose of PNEs was to build a network of dominant enterprises in the targeted sector and offer them better possibilities for further development like subsidies, easy access to transportation and raw materials and higher exchange retention rights. The PNEs had to improve quality and increase the amount of exports. The initial targeted areas were machinery and electronic products.

Favourable rights for exchange created as a result of exports were given to targeted sectors especially to foreign trade corporations who play crucial rule in the procurement and exports of China. (Panagariya, 2003, p. 4) The impact of this policy is difficult to evaluate but from the figure 8 it is obvious that the country has managed switching to production of value added goods.

Figure 8 - Changing export composition of China

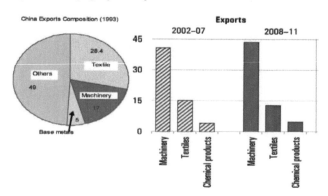

Source: IMF & CEIC (2009, p. 8)

23

FDI to China has played a key role in its export performance and overall economic growth. The effective policies of the government have attracted foreign investors to the country. For example 25% of foreign investment enables a company to get the status of joint venture and enjoy several tax exemptions. There is also no restriction on the choice of sectors to be invested or the minimum amount of investment. (Panagariya, 09.2003, p. 5)

Such kind of economic liberalization has lured lots of foreign companies into the country and increased the number of FIEs that have been responsible for 55% of exports and 53% of imports in 2010. From 2000 till 2009 China gained FDI flows more than any other developing country in the world. Currently China is also a big source of FDI and it took fourth place in the world for international mergers and acquisitions. (OECD, 2012, p. 54)

Another factor that has made Chinese exports successful is government credits offered to companies. The main bank of the country Bank of China gives credits and main receivers of these trade credits and foreign trade companies (FTC). In 1991 FTCs made up 85% of total credits.

Moreover, bank of China offers loans mainly to foreign enterprises. This liberal credit policy contributed to rapid growth of exports and attracted foreign investors to the local market. Hong-Kong has also played a crucial role in Chinese export success. In the mid 80s the entrepreneurs from Hong-Kong started to move their facilities and business to China because of cheap labour force and liberalization of Chinese business atmosphere. (Panagariya, 2003, p. 7) This process paved way to transfer of capital to China, brought modern management methods and connected China to the world market. In 1992 Hong-Kong possessed 70% of foreign investments to China. Hong-Kong till today has a big influence on exports in China. (Panagariya, 2003, p. 8)

Local policies of Chinese provinces in terms of support to enterprises and favourable conditions for them have proven to be effective. The economic system of China has been decentralized and the role of local regions and provinces has increased. It has led to better management of local economy and attraction of foreign enterprises to the regions. (Panagariya, 2003, p. 8)

The geographical location of China has also a big impact on export success and competitiveness of the country. The country exports heavy goods to near destinations and light goods to long distances. The nearness of export destinations enables China to get lower transportation costs. (Harrigan & Deng, 2010, p. 109) From the figure 9 it is obviously seen that many export destinations of China are geographically near to it.

Figure 9

China's top twenty export markets, 2006

	Distance from Beijing	Exports ($ billions)	% exports sent by air
United States	11,154	203	19
Hong Kong	1,979	155	12
Japan	2,102	92	15
Korea	956	45	14
Germany	7,829	40	33
The Netherlands	7,827	31	22
United Kingdom	8,146	24	15
Singapore	4,485	23	35
Taiwan	1,723	21	26
Italy	8,132	16	9
Russia	5,799	16	7
Canada	10,458	16	12
India	3,781	15	17
France	8,222	14	26
Australia	9,025	14	14
Malaysia	4,351	14	35
Spain	9,229	12	9
United Arab Emirates	5,967	11	7
Belgium	7,969	10	14
Thailand	3,301	10	16

Source: Harrigan & Deng (2010, p. 120)

According to CIA world factbook in 2012 the share of following countries in Chinese exports was: USA 17.2%, Hong Kong 15.8%, Japan 7.4%, and South Korea 4.3%. As it seems from the list the last three main export destinations are located near to China. (CIA world factbook China, 2014)

China has succeeded in a short time to raise the volume of its exports and get shares in world market. However, there emerges a question regarding the sustainability of this gigantic economy. According to IMF prognosis if China keeps moving forward under current export growth the real exports will grow annually around 14½ %. (Guo & N'Diaye, 2009, p. 10) The figure 10 shows future assessment of Chinese market share.

25

The figure 10 - Future assessment of Chinese market share

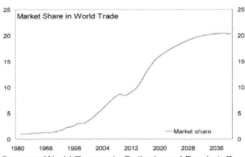

Sources: World Economic Outlook; and Fund staff
estimates.

Source: IMF (2009, p 10)

If the prognosis comes to be true then by 2040 China will have 20% of world exports doubling its current share. However, there are some pessimistic predictions regarding expansion of emerging markets especially China. (Guo & N'Diaye, 2009, p. 10) Palley (2011) have noted several predictions regardin negative impact of Chinese expansion on industrialized economies that are main export destinations of China. The author, including many other scientists believe that in order to provide economic sustainability and avoid of economical crisis in the world, the domestic demand of emerging markets should be increased. This issue will be discussed in the next chapters. (Palley, 2011, p. 19)

4.1 COMPETITIVENESS OF GERMANY AND CHINA

Germany takes the fourth place in the GCI 2013/2014 that could be considered as one of the most competitive countries in the world. The country ranked 3rd for the quality of infrastructure in the GCR. (GCR 2013/2014, p. 23)

The local market of the country is characterized with intense competition of companies; SMEs (German *Mittelstand*) play key role in the exports and growth of the country.

SMEs account for 52% of total economic output, employ 60% of workers and 19% of exports come to their share. (Federal ministry for economic affairs and energy of Germany, 2013, p. 3/9) Their existence and active participation in the economy makes local market more competitive. Many of these medium size companies have been leaders on their area and got share in the world market. They are called hidden champions of Germany and are considered to be backbone of German economy. 95% of German companies are family-owned (Federal ministry for economic affairs and energy of Germany, 2013, p. 4)

The enterprises of the country are innovative and employ latest technology in the production process (16th GCI). The large domestic market of Germany (5th) enables it to benefit from economies of scale and skilled labour force. There is still lack of quality of the educational system (23th) and the labour market remains tough. The bureaucratical problems like high costs of hiring an employer or firing from the job prevents the new job creations. Fortunately, the country improves the educational system periodically, which is driving engine behind innovation led economy. (GCR 2013/2014, p. 23)

Figure 11 - Germany according to GCI 2013/2014

Global Competitiveness Index

	Rank (out of 148)	Score (1–7)
GCI 2013–2014	**4**	**5.5**
GCI 2012–2013 (out of 144)	6	5.5
GCI 2011–2012 (out of 142)	6	5.4
Basic requirements (20.0%)	**9**	**5.9**
Institutions	15	5.3
Infrastructure	3	6.2
Macroeconomic environment	27	5.7
Health and primary education	21	6.4
Efficiency enhancers (50.0%)	**8**	**5.3**
Higher education and training	3	5.9
Goods market efficiency	21	4.9
Labor market efficiency	41	4.6
Financial market development	29	4.7
Technological readiness	14	5.7
Market size	5	6.0
Innovation and sophistication factors (30.0%)	**4**	**5.6**
Business sophistication	3	5.7
Innovation	4	5.5

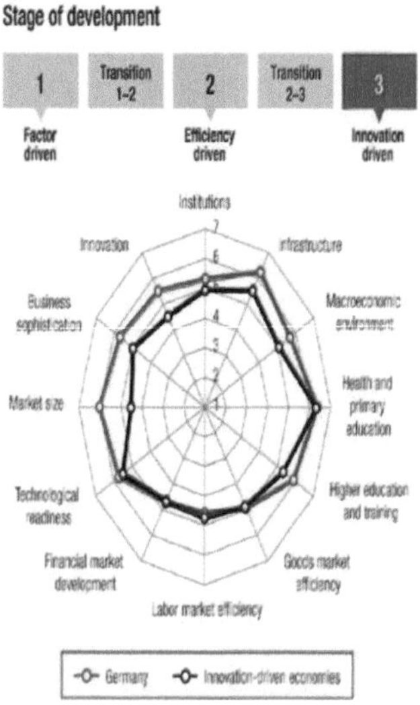

Source: GCR (2013/2014, p. 194)

The role of institutions in the growth and development of the economy is very important. Especially the recent financial crisis in the world economy and in Europe made it clear that the effective functioning of institutions is crucial factor for stability and growth. In the economic literature the institutions are mainly classified as private and public, however the latter has been mainly discussed. (GCI 2013/2014, p. 5) The government type of Germany is federal republic that consists of 16 states (*Bundesländer*) and the legality is based on civil law system. Germany has achieved relatively high level of democracy and it contributes to effective functioning of institutions.

The level of corruption is low and transparency of institution activities meets the standards. The biggest problem of public institutions as mentioned before is bureaucracy that creates artificial difficulties for different spheres of economy. In spite of the fact that there is a healthy business atmosphere in the country, the bureaucratical rules hinder increase of local and foreign investment to country. (CIA world factbook China, 2014)

Germany is one of the most effective countries in terms of quality of infrastructure. In general infrastructure includes many factors of economy but two main aspects play key role in competitiveness: transportation and communication network. The transportation facilities of the country include air, water and land. Hamburg is the second biggest port of Europe after Rotterdam and Duisburg is one of the biggest internal ports of the continent. The water system of the country connects 250 ports where Elbe and Rhine play important role. The existence of water transportation network enables the enterprises and other facilities to benefit from cheap delivery. Moreover, the air network of the country is also well developed and there are international flights from 23 airports of the country. Frankfurt is the world's 7th biggest cargo shipment and 9th biggest passenger airport. The length of railroads is about 37900 km and the trains can reach up to 300km/h speed. It is fourth biggest in the world. The length of the roadways is 645000 km and the country ranks 11th in the world. (GTAI, 2011)

Information and communication technology (ICT) currently is very important area of economy not only for Germany but also for the whole world. 80% of innovation in Germany is backed by ICT and the country has biggest ICT market in Europe and third largest in the world.

28

On this sphere Germany has been quite successful; however there are still challenges and pressure of competition from USA and Asian countries. (Federal Ministry of Education and Research, 2007, p. 4/8)

Macroeconomic stability alone cannot provide economic growth, however unstable macroeconomic environment can hinder the development of economy. The inflation rate, unemployment, GDP, national income, trade and etc are important macroeconomic factors that determine the competitiveness of the country. (GCR, 2013/2014, p. 6) The growth of GDP in Germany fluctuated between 0.3% and 0.7% in the quarters of 2013. In 2013, the GDP of the country made up 2.737,6 trillion Euros and this figure is quite high for a country with around 81 million population. (Destatis, 2013)

The employment rate in Germany is relatively positive and in January of 2014 the number of employed people reached 41.7 million. This is an increase of 297.000 or 0.7% in compare of previous year. The unemployment rate in January of 2014 was 5.6%. (Destatis, 2014) The inflation rate for 2013 has made up 1.5%. (Destatis, 2013) These figures make it clear that the macroeconomic situation in Germany is stable and there are few threats that can harm the growth of economy and exports.

Another very important factor of competitiveness is education quality of the country especially when there are limited natural resources the availability well educated labour force is vital. The key fact that surprised many experts regarding Germany was 0.6% increase of employment among people with tertiary education during world crisis between 2008 and 2009. (OECD, 2011, p. 2) Germany performs well in compare of previous years according to OECD education standards. 86% of people aged between 25 and 64 have got their high school degree and this indicator is higher than the average of OECD 74%.

In 2013 the average student of the country in the OECD programme PISA collected 510 points in maths, science and reading literacy outreaching the average of OECD 497. Moreover, Germany offers lower tuition fees for international students and it attracts many young people around the world to education system of Germany. After education some percentage of foreign students remains in the country and contribute to its economy.

29

Healthcare system is considered to be one of the advanced in the world and the life expectancy in the country is around 81 years. 81% of Germans are positive about their living conditions. (OECD better life index) As we see from GCI 2013/2014 the labour market efficiency is not high in Germany. The employment legislation of the country is not flexible and in this regard Germany performs less effective among OECD countries. (OECD, 2013, p. 1)

For example the dismissal process of the employee can be delayed by work council until the court makes final decision. The employers are not independent in selecting which worker to dismiss in the case of redundancy until meeting social requirements like proving that the certain worker cannot be kept in other position. Fortunately this difficult situation has been improved with the adoption of rules regarding the dismissal of the worker in case of redundancy. The employer by paying costs of dismissal and other unemployment benefits can easily solve the problem without court interference. Many experts have stated that the removal of strict employment regulations can positively impact on competitiveness of Germany. (OECD, 2013, p. 2)

Germany is ranked 5 according to the size of its market in the world and it is largest in Europe. (GCI, 2013/2014, p. 23) The country has bigger population and it accounts for 20% of European GDP. (GTAI, 2013, p. 5) In addition to above mentioned aspects of competitiveness the effective innovation is a driving engine of competitiveness. A firm or a country can survive in a globalizing economy only by upgrading and innovating its technologies. In this regard Germany has been successful and the term "Made in Germany" is understood in many countries as a synonym for quality and trust. The country ranks 4 in the GCI 2013/2014 according to innovation. Innovation itself is interdependent with education, R&D and they altogether constitute substantial part of competitiveness. In 2010 Germany spent 70 billion Euros on R&D making the larger investment on this sphere among European countries. (GTAI, 2013, p. 9)

In 2012 the R&D made up 2.98% of the GDP and this is one of the highest rates in the world. Around 34000 companies in Germany are involved in R&D activities and the high-tech strategy of the government is aimed at developing this area.

Germany Trade & Invest plays an important role in research activities and provide local enterprises with regarding international market and business possibilities. (Federal Ministry for Economic Affairs and Energy of Germany)

The main economic policy of the country "Ordnungspolitik" paves the way for improvement of competitiveness in Germany. The effective competition plays a key role in the formation of competitiveness. In spite of the some shortage in this respect, Germany has achieved high level of competitiveness and the companies are well adjusted to international competition posed by globalization process. Recently, Germany has achieved higher trade surplus and this is the result of effective competitiveness. (Federal Ministry of Economics and Technology of Germany, 2013, p. 7)

Above we mentioned the progress and development of Germany, however there are some shortages that hinder the economic growth. As it is seen from GCI the main economic problem of the country is linked to taxation. This problem has been covered also in the report of OECD (2012). The labour taxation is high 39% in compare of OECD average of 24%. In addition the high level of social contributions serves as a disincentive for employers and could be an obstacle in immigration of highly skilled labour force. It is believed that lowering of social contributions especially for low income workers can contribute to increase of employment. Therefore the reform in the taxation system of Germany is considered to be one of major issues. (OECD, 2012, p. 10)

The labour regulations are regarded to be an obstacle preventing the growth rate of employment. It has been mainly criticized for its rigidity and less incentives for employers. Another problem bureaucracy causes additional budget expenditures and affects the competition negatively. (Federal Ministry of Economics and Energy of Germany, 2012, p. 47)

However recent policies of government have much focused on removal of bureaucracy and it has already yielded some results. The blue card system that has been applied to attract highly skilled labour force from foreign countries seems to be effective. Apart from it the regulations for foreign workers have been mitigated. (Federal Ministry of Economics and Energy of Germany, 2012, p. 42) Bureaucracy reduction and better regulation program made the regulatory requirements flexible contributing to effective time and costs management.

31

It is worth to mention the fact that bureaucracy reduction policy on the business sphere made it possible to save 11 billion Euros in the period between 2006 and 2011. (Federal Ministry of Economics and Energy of Germany, 2012, p. 48)

Figure 12 – Main problems hindering business in Germany

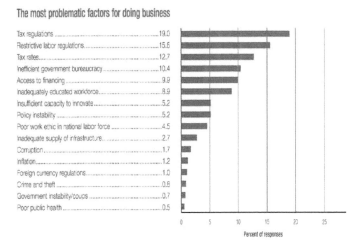

Source: GCI (2013/2014, p. 194)

China has been ranked 29th in the GCI 2013-2014. As we see from the below-shown figure the overall competitiveness of the country is not enough strong in many aspects. The macroeconomic situation and labour market efficiency are relatively well positioned. Technological readiness of the country does not meet high standards meaning that the majority of the enterprises are not well equipped with latest technologies. In terms of innovation China has been making progress and invests much on research and development. Another factor that makes China competitive is its huge market enabling to benefit from economies of scale and attract FDI to the country. (GCI, 2013/2014, p. 34)

The institutions of the country are not well effective in terms of corruption and bureaucracy. The corruption rate is quite high in the country that negatively impacts on internal competition. (Lawrence, 2013, p 18/24) In 2013 the country has ranked 80 by Transparency International according to corruption level. (Transparency International)

Figure 13 - China according to 12 pillars of GCI 2013/2014

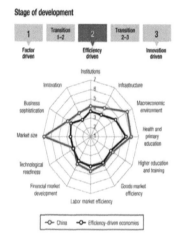

Source: GCI (2013/2014, p. 156)

In spite of the fact that China does not perform well according to GCI factors it has been able to be the largest exporter in the world. The reason of this success is not only cheap labour force or lower exchange rate, but also capability to meet the demand of the world. (Adams et al, 2004, p. 29) From this perspective, the FDI plays crucial role in competitiveness of China. In 1990s the country was mainly exporting low quality products but after foreign intervention mainly from Taiwan and Hong Kong the situation changed dramatically. Furthermore western countries were lured into country to benefit from cheap labour force. (Adams et al, 2004, p. 24) They used China as a chain of production and also exported to huge internal market of the country. The establishment of factories and other entities in China enabled to raise the level of technology.

The spill-over effect contributed to this process and local enterprises improved their capabilities. As a result of large FDI flows into the country the quality of products has improved considerably and China has been able to enter world markets. The share of high technology in Chinese exports increase annually. (Adams et al, 2004, p. 25)

Low wages and existence of huge number of labour force is another aspect of Chinese competitiveness. For example the average hourly salary of Chinese worker is 0.81 dollars that make 2.7% of American employee wage. The rural areas of the country have even lower wages than bigger cities and there is a strong migration of labour force to economic centres. Periodically, the wages in the country increase and it causes concerns about sustainability of competitiveness. The workers of many companies organize often strikes demanding higher salaries and better work conditions. Honda raised the salary of workers 47% after intensive strikes. Another problem regarding Chinese labour force is declining population as a result of one child policy. The government has recently relaxed the law allowing more children for some groups of the society. (wordpress, 2012)

The macroeconomic situation in China is relatively stable and it makes country attractive for FDI. The GDP (exchange rate) of China for 2013 was around 8.939 trillion US dollars. The annual growth rate of GDP in the same period made up 7.6%. The inflation rate in 2013 was 2.6% and unemployment rate 6.4%. (CIA world factbook China) The GDP grows steadily and according to IMF estimates in 2016 it will constitute 11.779.979 billion US dollars. (IMF)

In terms of innovation China has made progress, however it is not considered to be among top innovators in the world. As it is mentioned above the impact of Taiwan, Hong Kong and western countries paved a way for further development of innovation in the country. Currently, China is not only production chain of the bigger multinational companies but also the local companies have already started to distinguish with their innovation capabilities. This is the result of government policy to enhance innovation in the country.

34

Since 2009 China is the second largest land in terms of expenditures on R&D after United States. It is predicted that the GDP expenditures on innovation will constitute 2.5% making China top innovative country. (OECD, 2012, p. 264)

China has ranked 48th in the GCI 2013/2014 according to quality of infrastructure which plays crucial role in the development of any economy. There are 507 airports in China and in this regard the country takes 14th place in the world. The length of roadways is 4.106.387 km and the railroad is 86000 km. According to the length of waterways China ranks first in the world with 110000 km length. There are many large sea ports in the east coast of the country, which are capable to receive and dispatch millions of containers. (CIA world factbook China) China invests heavily on road transportation (61%) as this type of infrastructure is mainly used both for passenger and load carriage. (Li & Fung, 2012, p. 4) There are still major problems regarding infrastructure of the country because the connection between east and the west of the country is not well developed. (Li & Fung, 2012, p. 44)

The education in China develops gradually and the number of graduates increases annually. In 2009 less that 5% had a tertiary education, which is far below from OECD average 30%. It is estimated that currently around 65% of young people will finish upper secondary education; however it is again below OECD average of 82%. (OECD, 2011, p. 2) The public expenditures on education in China make up 16.3%, which is higher, that many countries including US with 13.8%. Nonetheless as a percentage of GDP expenditures on education are not high. (OECD, 2011, p. 3) The number of Chinese students studying abroad is high and 18.2% of all foreign students enrolled at OECD countries are from China. This is the largest international student group at OECD countries. The majority of Chinese students (21.9%) have been enrolled in the USA. (OECD, 2011, p. 4) The various regions of China have also different education performance. For instance, Shanghai has scored 17 points more than long term leader in PISA ranking Finland. (OECD, 2011, p. 6)

The financial system of China differs from the western market based financial system with its specific features: the state ownership, domination of banks for business financing, closed system and the dynamic economic growth.

The banks of China are responsible for 90% of financing for commercial enterprises. The state plays important role in financial system. For instance the state has controlling stakes at 5 major commercial banks and 100% at the three policy banks. These main banks have around half of bank assets. (Bell & Chao, 2010, p. 4).

Figure 14: The share of state in the financial system of China

	Total Assets*		State Ownership*
	RMB	US$	
Top Five Banks	(in billions)		
Industrial and Commercial Bank of China	9,757.2	$ 1,434.9	51%
China Construction Bank	7,555.5	1,111.0	48%
Agricultural Bank of China	7,100.0	1,044.1	100%
Bank of China	6,951.7	1,022.3	70.8%
Bank of Communications	268.3	39.5	26%
Three Policy Banks			
China Development Bank	3,821.2	$ 561.9	100%
Agricultural Development Bank of China	1,354.7	199.2	100%
Export-Import Bank of China	566.7	83.3	100%

*Source: 2008 Annual Reports

Source - Bell & Chao (2010, p. 4)

The strict state regulation on financial system lowers the efficiency of the system. In contrast market based system can enhance efficiency and competition. (Bell & Chao, 2010, p. 22) The strong involvement of the state into banking sector generates moral hazard. The bank shareholders will take higher risks and be less worried about the management quality relying on the support of the state in case of crisis. Another point is "too big to fail" policy that makes bank sector confident regarding state support. The major banks believe that government will never allow them to fail as it can cause big financial problems.

The conditions for entrance of foreign financial institutions into financial system of China are not favourable as the state owned banks have more government support. (Bell & Chao, 2010, p. 23)

China opens gradually its financial market to foreign investments and moreover the huge financial institutions of the country are becoming challenge for foreign institutions. (Bell & Chao, 2010, p. 24)

The top 3 problems of China in terms of competitiveness according to GCI (2013-2014) are access to financing, inefficient government bureaucracy and corruption. There are mainly bigger barriers for SMEs to access the financial resources in China. However, SMEs play significant role for Chinese economy as they make up 55.6% of GDP, 62.3% of exports and 75% of employment. The main reasons for these obstacles: 1) high credit risk 2) insufficiency of collateral assets 3) shortage of information.

Credit risk attributes failure of the borrower to give back any type of credit. The trust of banks or other financial institutions who lend money on SMEs is low as it is believed that they are under tough competition and their profit is small. Moreover, SMEs have lower management qualities as they have been established in a short period of time and the probability of their default is high. (Silburt, 2012, p. 2) In the case if the credit rating of SME is not enough to get a loan its collateral assets will be considered. However, in most cases they don't have enough properties or other type of assets to offer against loss. Shortage of information regarding the borrower makes banks less interested in issuing a loan.

The information regarding management quality, business plan and reputation can be beneficial in building trustful relation between banks and borrowers. Such kind of information asymmetry occurs mainly because of poor management capabilities of SMEs and the intention to hide information for tax purposes. (Silburt, 2012, p. 3) The root of these problems is improper state intervention and inefficient financial system regulation. (Silburt, 2012, p. 4) In order to solve these problems it is recommended to decrease state interference to financial system, to develop collaboration between banks and borrowers and follow credit based system for loans. (Silburt, 2012, p. 8)

The bureaucracy in China is an obstacle for the growth of economy. The source of this problem is related to the government that is controlled mainly by communist party. The coordination among state institutions is not effective and it results with competition between state entities.

37

Main disputes arise because of jurisdiction over certain issue, budget resource allocation and recognition from higher officials. (Lawrence & , 2013, p. 14)

Bureaucratic rank system is key feature of Chinese political structure. The public institutions, agencies and other state entities interact with each other according to their ranks. This rank hierarchy in turn damages the cooperation among institutions and reaching effective coordination. The entities having the same rank cannot give mandatory orders to each other. To do so they have to apply higher instances like communist party or security agencies. The institution with lower rank has few chances to reach an institution with higher rank in order to cooperate. (Lawrence & 2013, p. 15) The government has initiated several programs to remove rank system however it has been opposed by many officials. The ministers or other high ranking officials are receiving expensive cars, houses and other privileges from the state.

Such kind of bureaucracy hinders the cooperation not only between domestic agencies but also with international institutions. (Lawrence & 2013, p. 16) The rule of law is weak in China and the country seems unable to enforce and implement laws and regulation fully. The main reason is the central communist party who has concentrated the power in its hands. The party is unwilling to accept restrictions generated from the rule of law and keeps itself above the law. (Lawrence & 2013, p. 17)

Corruption is not unusual phenomenon in China and widespread all over the country. It includes expensive gifts, corporate shares and stakes offered to officials in return for permits, approvals, jobs and exemption of laws and rules. (Lawrence & 2013, p. 18) The scale of corruption has grown in accordance with economic growth. According to estimations of Chinese central bank, corrupt officials who fled abroad between 1990 and 2008 took with them 120 billion US dollars.

The report of Global financing Integrity – Washington based research centre – in 2012 estimated, the illegal financial flows out of China between 2001 and 2010 2.74 trillion US dollars.

38

In 2012 after appointment as communist party general secretary Xi Jinping determined corruption inside the party as main problems. He promised to combat against corruption together with his comrades. However, the self-control within the party does not yield effective results. The major organisation fighting the corruption Central Discipline Inspection Commission is politically under pressure and their inspections don't end with true results. It has been recommended to increase the role of media in combating the corruption, however such kind of proposals have not been accepted yet. In spite of this fact the political activists disclose the property and assets of Chinese officials in internet. (Lawrence & , 2013, p. 19) The figure 15 describes main problems hindering the business in China.

Figure 15 - Obstacles for business in China

The most problematic factors for doing business

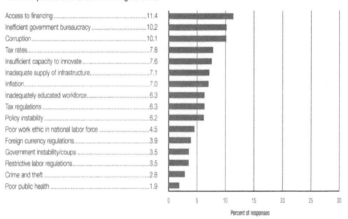

Note: From the list of factors above, respondents were asked to select the five most problematic for doing business in their country and to rank them between 1 (most problematic) and 5. The bars in the figure show the responses weighted according to their rankings.

Source: GCI (2013/14, p. 158)

4.2 THE EXPORTS OF GERMANY TO RUSSIA

The trade and economic collaboration have been traditionally regarded an important part of German-Russian relationship. Even after the end of Second World War the trade started to revive with both "FRG" and "GDR". These both German countries together made up one fifth of Soviet foreign trade. In 70s "Mannesmann AG" agreed to deliver wide diameter pipes needed for construction of gas pipeline from Siberia to Europe in exchange for gas. The project was funded by" Deutsche Bank AG" whose representative office was one of the first opened in Moscow in 1973. Another contract was signed between "Ruhrgas AG" and "Soyuzgazexport" that aimed to provide 40 billion cubic meters gas to Germany in 25 years. In agreement with the project "Mannesmann AG" was responsible for not only supply of pipelines but also equipment for gas production and its transportation.

These past projects currently are the basement of energy resource delivery to Europe. After collapse of Soviet Union and reunification of Germany the trade turnover between countries decreased. In 1998, financial crisis in Russia that caused rapid devaluation of rouble and increasing import prices again negatively affected the trade relationship. (Pakhomov & Cramon-Taubadel, 2013, p. 13) The situation improved in 2004 and Germany became the leading exporter in Russian market. Since then the trade has developed dynamically, however in 2009 there was a decline as a result of world financial crisis. In spite of this fact German companies kept increasing their activity in Russia and by the end of 2010 the number of German companies registered in Russia reached 6100. (Pakhomov & Cramon-Taubadel, 2013, p. 14)

Germany currently is one of the main suppliers of machinery, equipment and consumption products to Russian market. (DIHK, .2011, p. 2) In terms of investment Germany is regarded one of the main partners of Russia. The major investor companies from Germany are: "E.ON" (electricity), "KNAUF" (construction material), "METRO" (hypermarket), and "VOLKSWAGEN" (automobile production). (Pakhomov & Cramon-Taubadel, 2013, p. 19)

Germany takes sixth place according to the amount of accumulated investment to Russia with 19.5 billion Euros in 2012. (GTA & AHK, 2013, p. 8)

40

In 2012 Germany was the third largest trade partner of Russia behind the Netherlands and China. The figure below shows trade volume of Germany with Russia in different periods:

Table 1 - German-Russian Trade

Germany→Russia (in billion US dollars)	2007	2008	2009	2010	2011	2012
Exports	26.5	34.1	21.2	26.7	37.7	38.3
Imports	26.3	33.2	18.7	25.1	34.2	35.6

Source: Federal Customs Service of Russia

The trade volume for January-September of 2013 made up 57.9 billion Euros and out of it 27.4 billion Euros are exports from Germany to Russia and the rest imports of Germany from Russia. (Trade and economic office of Russian embassy in Berlin, 2013, p. 1) In 2013 the share of Russia in German exports made up 3.4% and Russia takes 11th place in terms of German export destination. In terms of German imports Russia is the 7th country who mainly supplies energy resources. (Trade and economic office of Russian embassy in Berlin, 2013, p. 2) German exports to Russia mainly consist of Automobiles and its parts, machinery, chemical products and etc. (Trade and economic office of Russian embassy in Berlin, 2013, p. 3) The list below shows main export products of Germany to Russia in 2013:

- Automobile and its parts (21.3%)
- Machinery (11.9%)
- Pharmaceutical products (5.2%)
- Chemical products (5%)
- Electro-technical industry (4.4%)
- Electrical industry (4%)
- Other products (3.9%) (Trade and economic office of Russian embassy in Berlin, 2013, p.14)

If look at the overall import products of Russia it is obviously seen that the share of machinery and technology is big.

The figure 16 describes the share of certain products in entire imports of Russia (2011).

Figure 16 - Russian imports 2011

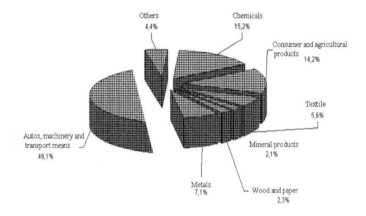

Source: Kobrina & Lixachev (2011, p. 60)

According to GCI (2013-2014) Russia takes 59th place in terms technological readiness. The above mentioned figure shows that Russia strives to modernize its technological capability through imports of high technologies. In this regard there are many opportunities for German companies in Russia who can provide local market with innovative products. As it was previously mentioned the main import product of Russia from Germany is automobile and its components. Since 2007 "VW" have started production in Kaluga city 170 km from Moscow. (VW)

The leader of Russian automobile market is "VW" after the "AwtoWAZ-Renault-Nissan". In 2012 "VW" sold 316.264 autos, which are 38% more than the year 2011. The concern plans to invest more in production and increase the capacity up to 225.000 till 2016. (DIHK, 2012, p. 24) Almost half of automobiles in Russia are 12 years old and there is a necessity to replace them with new ones. In 2012 there were 42.5 million automobiles in Russian roads and it accounts for 300 autos for 1000 people.

It is expected that the number of autos in Russia will rise up to 50 million making the ratio 35/1000. (DIHK, 2012, p. 25) In Germany there are 564 autos for 1000 people and in the USA the number is even more. In order protect its local automobile production Russia takes some measures like enforcement of utilization duties for imported automobiles in September of 2012, which resulted, with decrease of automobile imports. (DIHK, 2012, p. 26)

Table 2 - The list and value of exported German products to Russia

	Export from Germany to Russia		%
	January- September 2012	January- September 2013	2013
Name	Mln.euros		%
Automobile and engines	4342,81	3442,34	12,5
Other parts and accessories for autos	1 745,49	1 768,97	6,4
Pharmaceutical products	1 263,02	1 416,36	5,2
Other products	1 136,65	1 066,90	3,9
Machinery without specialization	719,70	730,92	2,7
Machinery for construction and its components	762,09	635,99	2,3
Control and measure equipment	635,89	643,06	2,3

Source: economic and trade office of Russian embassy in Berlin (2013, p. 12)

The entrance of Russia to WTO in 2012 is expected to ease the access of German products to Russia and in accordance with membership the import duties have to diminish from 10 to 7.8% by 2020. For industrial products import duties will be reduced even more from 9.4 to 6.4%. The duties for new automobiles are expected to be reduced from 25 to 15% by 2019. (DIHK, 2011, p. 2) The import duties currently in average have decreased from 9.6 up to 7.5%. These changes have been attributed to food products like meat, vegetables, fruits and etc.

43

The duties for household equipment and electro-technology have remained unchanged. It will be modified gradually. (DIHK, 2012, p. 54) The Russian localisation policy aims mainly improving its competitiveness in the world by attracting investment to the country. German companies are actively participating in the establishment of manufacture facilities in Russia, including the large firms like auto tyre producer "Continental", machine tool builder "Gildemeister AG", medicine manufacturer "Paul Hartmann". The main geographical areas to be invested by German enterprises are St. Petersburg, Kaluga and the territory around Volga. (DIHK, 2012, p. 58)

The eastern part of Russia is also lucrative place for German enterprises; but the poor infrastructure hinders the active investment to these areas. In this respect north-west of Russia are more attractive and the majority of investment are accumulated there. Since 2007 "Bosch-Siemens" produce "Strelna" refrigerators in the suburbs of St. Petersburg and have recently established production line for washing machines. (DIHK, 2012, p. 60) The image of Germany among Russian companies is high and "Made in Germany" is perceived as an equivalent of quality. German engineers hold higher positions in Russian factories like steel concern "Kirovskij Zavod". (DIHK, 2012, p. 61)

72% of German imports from Russia make up oil and gas. (Trade and economic office of Russian embassy in Berlin, 2013, p 14) It buys 40% of its natural gas and 30% of oil from Russia. Germany plans to leave nuclear power by 2022 and after this period there might be energy deficits in the country. This opens many opportunities and possibilities for Russian energy exports to Germany until the alternative energy resources provide the country with enough electricity. (Librondt, 2013, p. 14)

However, the exports of Germany to Russia and overall trade between countries are negatively affected by several factors. The major problem that German companies are confronted is higher rate of corruption, lack of qualified workforce and government bureaucracy. According to corruption level Russia ranks 136th out of 176 countries in the assessment of transparency international. The oligarchs play key role in the Russian economy and they have bigger influence on overall situation of the country.

The politics have also a big impact on entire economic relationships between Germany and Russia. Therefore the factor of political relations is taken into consideration while researching the export performance of Germany in Russia. (Librondt, 2013, p. 15) Germany after the Second World War pursues mainly diplomacy based policy and avoids major military confrontation with any country. The Political relationship with Russia is based on "change through integration" policy. It includes realization of common projects and establishment of institutions aimed to build effective economic relationship, develop democracy and rule of law in Russia, and cooperate in different spheres. Such kind of attitude has not yet yielded expected results, however at the moment there is not better alternative policy towards Russia. (Librondt, 2013, p. 18)

The political conflict over the future of Ukraine between EU and Russia has further strained the relations. The survey conducted by German-Russian foreign trade chamber among 105 German companies working in Russia has shown that 39% of firms are concerned about the negative impact of political processes on their business. (*Deutsch-Russische AH*, 2014, p. 1) The 2014 winter Olympic Games in Sotschi gave a positive impulse on exports of German exports to Russia. Around 100 mainly medium-size firms were involved in preparation for Olympic Games and their services are valued in billions. (*Deutsch-Russische AH*, 2014, p. 2)

The current business atmosphere in Russia is considered lightly positive developing. According to inquiry of German-Russian foreign trade chamber and East Committee of German Economy in 2013 among German companies engaged in Russia revealed that 50% of firms are positive about changes in business atmosphere. (*Deutsch-Russische AHK & OA der Deutschen Wirtschaft, 2013,* p. 3) Moreover, the survey also covered the opinion of companies regarding advantages and disadvantages of Russian market. The figure 17 describes the opinion of German companies operating in Russia about market situation in the country.

Figure 17 - Survey among German companies operating in Russia

What are the advantages and disadvantages of Russian market?

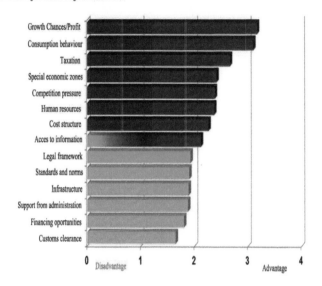

Source: *Deutsch-Russische AHK/OA der Deutschen Wirtschaft (2013,* p. 12)

In spite of the fact that, there are many obstacles for German companies in Russia there is bigger interest for market of the largest country in the world. (Librondt, 2013, p. 17)

4.3 THE EXPORTS OF CHINA TO RUSSIA

Before the Second World War the trade relations between China and Russia were not well established, because of low transport connections and hard political situation in both countries. During 1920s and 1930s China made up 3-5% of Soviet Union's trade. (Moshes & Nojonen, 2011, p. 41) After establishment of Chinese People Republic in 1949 with the great support of Soviet Union the trade relations started to develop rapidly.

The similar economic system of the countries was another factor that fostered trade between them. In 1950s China accounted for 15-20% of Soviet Union's foreign trade and the relations were further strengthened as a result of confrontation with the west. Soviet Union accounted for 40% of Chinas foreign trade in 1960s. However, the trade between countries did not grow furthermore due to political disputes and competition in the communistic area. The peak of trade failure was reached in 1969 after the border conflict and the trade was almost stopped. The situation was to some extend improved after Gorbachev came into power.

The collapse of Soviet Union opened new page in the trade relations of Russia and China. In the 1990s the situation in Russia was strained due to internal conflicts and transition to a new economic system. The decrease in oil prices further worsened economic stability in Russia and in 1998 the country was confronted with financial crisis. The ongoing negative economic processes in Russia prevented development of trade with China. (Moshes & Nojonen, 2011, p. 42) The economic recovery of Russia started in 2000s accompanied with economic growth of China. As the economy of China grew its demand for raw materials increased simultaneously and this enabled Russia to raise its exports of crude oil and gas. Consequently, the exports of Russia increased 4 times from $5 billion up to $20 billion during 2000-2010. In short period of time the imports from China reached 17% in compare of 3% in 2000s. Currently China is the biggest exporter in Russian market and bigger importer of Russian raw materials. (Moshes & Nojonen, 2011, p. 43)

The share of Russia as a trade partner of China was 1.96% in 2001 and it did not change significantly since then constituting 2% in 2011. In the beginning of decade China was lagging behind some EU members, CIS countries, USA and Japan according to trade volume with Russia, however in 2011 it was already the first trade partner of Russia. (Alexandrovich, 2012, p. 1) China made up 6.8% of Russian exports and 15.8% of imports in 2011. The share of raw material mainly crude oil in the exports of Russia to China increased from 10.9% in 2001 up to 63.4% in 2011. Timber and wood products comprise 12.3 % of Russian exports. (Alexandrovich, 2012, p. 2) In contrast China exports mainly machinery and technology to Russia.

Figure 18 - The share of certain export products from China to Russia

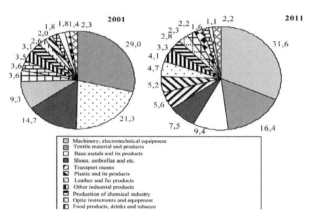

Source: Alexandrovich (2012, p. 5) referred to CEIC data

In compare of 2001 the share of machinery and equipment in the imports of Russia from China increased from 9.3% up to 31.6% in 2011. In the same period the value of delivered machinery and equipment grew from $0.25 billion up to $12.56 billion. The reason of growing machinery exports from China to Russia is explained with two factors: relocation of electrical and heavy industry from developed countries to China and the quality improvement of local producers. (Alexandrovich, 2012, p. 6) The share of transport means has also grown from 0.9% in 2001 up to 5.6% in 2011. The value of transport means has increased 92 times from $0.024 up to $2.2 billion in the same period. The essential part of transport means are road transportation which share constituted 83% in 2011. The increase of road transportation in the imports is explained with improvement of product characteristics and relatively cheaper price. (Alexandrovich, 2012, p. 7) Another major import product from China is textile goods which have increased significantly from 2001.

The share of this industry decreases periodically as China shifts mainly to production of value added goods. (Alexandrovich, 2012, p.5) The share of basic metals has grown from 1.8% ($0.05 billion) in 2001 up to 9.4% in 2011. The main part of this import consists of products made from basic metals.

48

Chemical products also make up essential part of Russian imports and their portion has reached 8.5% in 2011. (Alexandrovich, 2012, p. 5) In spite of the fact that the Russian exports to China are not prominent, the imports from China make up essential part of Russian market. 67% of shoes, 65% of light industry products (toys, bags and etc), 64% of various metallic goods, 60% of clothes, 54% of ceramic goods, 50% of office machinery and equipment, 38% of various industrial products, 35% of fabric, 32% of telecommunication equipment, 22% of electrical equipment come to share of imports from China. (Alexandrovich, 2012, p. 9)

Table 3 - The main products exported from China to Russia

Name	January-December of 2012		Change
	Import volume (mln.dol)	Share in overall import %	relatively to previous year 2011 %
Machinery and equipment including:	**18691.72**	**42.43**	**+17.45**
Electrical machinery and equipment	5942.29	13.49	+11.49
Energy, technological and other equipment, pumps, machines and etc	8506.20	19.31	+17.62
Automobiles, tractors and other transport means	2846.41	6.46	+34
Fur and its products	**1568.40**	**3.56**	**+37.62**
Shoes	**2600.38**	**5.90**	**+5.44**
Knitted wear	**2185.86**	**4.96**	**+8.01**
Textile clothes	**2121.89**	**4.82**	**+0.9**
Chemical products	**3858.58**	**8.76**	**+6.91**
Plastic and its products	1357.11	3.08	+8.55
Organic-chemical compound	601.50	1.36	+10.77

Source: Trade representation of RF in PRC (2012, p. 2/3)

49

In January-December of 2013 the trade turnover between Russia and China reached 89.212.69 million US dollars and out of it $39617.85 mln (-10.3 %) are Russian exports to China and $49594.84 mln (+12.6 %) are imports from China. (MEDR, Internet Portal of Foreign Economic relations of Russia)

Table 4 - The exports of China to Russia (January-December)

(*mln US dollars)

Year	Current period	Previous year	Growth (%)
2003	6034.55	3520.63	+71.4
2004	9106.75	6034.55	+50.9
2005	13212.2	9106.75	+45.2
2006	15832.43	13212.2	+19.8
2007	284488.48	15832.43	+79.9
2008	33005.43	284488.48	+15.9
2009	17513.77	33005.43	-47.1
2010	29612.52	17513.77	+69
2011	38903.83	29612.52	+31.4
2012	44057.53	38903.83	+13.2
2013	49594.84	44057.53	+12.6

Source: MEDR, Internet Portal of Foreign Economic relations of Russia

Another important factor in the economic relations of China and Russia is investments. Russia is interested in attracting Chinese investment mainly to far-east of the country which economically lags behind the western part. During last 8 years till 2012 the investment from China to Russia increased 40 times reaching 4.9 billion US dollar. The amount of investment rose more 250 million US dollars in the first 7 months of 2013. Russian Prime Minister Dmitry Medvedev invited Chinese investors to his country and encouraged them with state support while visiting China in 2013 October. According to him big Chinese companies invest mainly on energy sector, chemicals and mining, while the medium and small size firms are engaged mainly in agriculture and other spheres. (Xinhua News Agency, 2013)

The trade between Russia and China is expected to grow furthermore reaching 100 billion US dollars by 2015. Russia seeks to increase trade with China by 15% about it told the president Vladimir Putin in the summit of Asia-Pacific Economic Cooperation (APEC) summit in October of 2013. The president mentioned about ongoing infrastructure projects between countries. It is also expected that China's state-owned gas company PetroChina plans to invest 10 Billion US dollar on Russian gas fields. Moreover, there is agreed a project aiming to establish BRICS development bank with $100 billion dollars capital which will be rival of IMF and World Bank. (Russia Today News Website, 2013)

The accession of Russia to WTO on 22 August of 2012 opens new opportunities for Chinese exports. (Kumar, 2013, p. 23) In the framework of WTO membership Russia is obliged to remove the barriers for trade, prevent protectionism, discrimination and other factors hindering the access of foreign business to internal market. (Kumar, 2013, p. 24) According to new membership the import tariffs will be decreased averagely up to 7.8%. (Kumar, 2013, p. 25) Russia will charge the same railway freight for imported products taking into consideration the monopolistic status of Russian Railways. Moreover, the state will subsidize gas supplies only for households not for commercial enterprises. (Kumar, 2013, p. 26) Periodically the transparency and rule of law under WTO supervision are expected to strengthen which will lead to increase of Chinese investment and exports to Russian market. Actually Chinese products are competitive in Russian market and further liberalisation contributes to the growth of trade between countries. Moreover, the local Russian companies are also expected to benefit from liberalisation having a chance to import machinery in order to raise productivity. (Kumar, 2013, p. 27)

There are also some obstacles that hinder the trade between China and Russia. The legal structure of Russia and institutional problems affects negatively to mutual trade and FDI. It is very important to provide foreign investors and businessmen with legal support so that they enjoy equal rights with local firms.

As it was mentioned before the infrastructure of Russia is underdeveloped and this in turn has a negative impact on trade flows. The improvement of infrastructure can foster the bilateral trade and increase the role of Russia as a transit country.

51

Apart from it, the next step of Russian state could be informing the local companies about WTO and its system so that they adjust their policies under WTO. Another problem that presents negative outcomes for bilateral trade is "grey customs". There are illegal flows of goods in the border of Russia and China which damages the economy of countries. Therefore establishment of joint committees or institutions to combat illegal trade is considered to be very important issue. (Kumar, 2013, p. 28)

4.4 COMPETITION OF GERMAN AND CHINESE FIRMS IN RUSSIAN MARKET

As it was mentioned in previous sections China won leadership over Russian market in 2010 and since then it is the first trade partner of Russia. Below it is shown table 5 and 6 that describe the growth rate of trade between Germany-Russia and China-Russia in different periods.

Table 5 - Trade between China and Russia (January-December; mln US dollars)

	Trade turnover		RF Export to PRC		Import of RF from PRC	
	Amount	Growth (%)	Amount	Growth (%)	Amount	Growth (%)
2003	15760.62	+32,1	9726.07	+15.7	6034.55	+71.4
2004	21232.1	+34.7	12126.58	+24.7	9106.75	+50.9
2005	29103.1	+34.1	15890.9	+31.0	13212.2	+45.2
2006	33386.55	+14.7	17554.12	+10.5	15832.43	+19.8
2007	48165.37	+44.3	19676.89	+12.1	28488.48	+79.9
2008	56830.54	+18.0	23825.11	+21.0	33005.43	+15.9
2009	38796.72	+31.8	21282.95	-10.7	17513.77	-47.1
2010	55448.79	+43.1	25836.26	+21.7	29612.52	+69.0
2011	79249.30	+42.7	40345.47	+55.6	38903.83	+31.4
2012	88158.03	+11.2	44100.51	+9.2	44057.53	+13.2
2013	81076.00	+0.5	39617.85	-10.3	49594.84	+12.6

Source: Internet Portal of Foreign Trade, MEDR

Table 6 - Trade between Germany and Russia (billion US dollars)

Trade turnover   RF Export to FRG   Import of RF from FRG

	Amount	Growth (%)	Amount	Growth (%)	Amount	Growth (%)
2004	29.2	114.5	14.8	110.4	14.4	119
2006	43.0	130.2	24.5	124.1	18.5	139.1
2007	24.5	123.1	26.3	107.5	26.5	143.7
2008	18.5	127.2	33.2	125.9	34.1	128.6
2009	39.9	59.4	18.7	56.4	21.2	62.2
2010	51.8	129.7	25.1	134.2	26.7	125.8
2011	71.9	137.2	34.2	133.1	37.7	141.1
2012	73.9	102.9	35.6	104.8	38.3	101.6

Source: Internet Portal of Foreign Trade. MEDR

There are many factors that explain why China is winning in the Russian market. For example the share of China has significantly increased in the construction machinery delivery to Russia. In the mid 1990s and beginning of 2000s the construction machinery production in China was mainly aimed providing the local market. As the production increased the necessity to export emerged. Currently, apart from 10-20% price difference, the Chinese construction machinery also distinguishes with its quality. Shortly said the products constitute the mixture of quality and price. The tough internal competition and also pressure from European producers push Chinese manufacturers to improve the quality. According to estimations of Russian experts soon the construction machinery of China will make up 5-10% of all construction machinery in Russia. (Starsenal)

The same situation is observed in the sphere of transport means. The number of Chinese autos and trucks exported to Russian market grow periodically. The truck producers like "HOWO", "Dong Feng", "CAMC", "FAW", "FOTON", "SHAANXI" are already popular among Russian customers. These Chinese firms benefit from technological accomplishments of their European and Japanese counterparts. For example "HOWO" trucks are produced according to technology of "Volvo", "Dong Feng" with "Nissan", "CAMC" with "Mitsubishi".

53

The qualitative spare parts of Japanese and Western manufacturers like "Isuzu" and "Perkins" are used in the production of Chinese trucks. Another factor that makes Chinese producers successful in Russian market is low exploitation costs. The service of delivered machines and needed parts are provided relatively for lower prices. The role of geographical location also has an impact on distribution of certain machines. European firms are successful in the western part of Russia in terms of machine delivery and Chinese products are well spread in the eastern part of Russia including Siberia. The border between Russia and China in the Far East makes it easy for import of machines and the costs of delivery are also lower. (CBC, 2006)

The export of automobiles from China to Russia increases annually. There are produced around 20 millions automobiles in China yearly and 3% out of them are exported to different countries. In 2012 the number of Chinese cars exported to Russia reached 100000 doubling the figures of previous years. According to results of 2012 Chinese cars demonstrated bigger growing tempo in Russian market. In the same period Russian customers had 52.8 thousand Chinese cars which are 88.5% more than previous year. It is expected that in the coming years the number of Chinese cars will grow in Russian market. (Avtostat)

There are several reasons making China successful in Russian market. First of all, as it was mentioned before the mixture of improving quality and price make Chinese products attractive. Another important factor is geographical location of China which border directly with Russia. The increase of Chinese exports to Russia is also explained via improving infrastructure in the border regions. For example new opened rail way "Xhunchun-Kamishovaya" will contribute to the growth of trade flows up to 8 million tons. The construction of "Amur" bridge will further raise amount of trade up to 20 million tons annually. (Alterna International Trade Company, 2014)

According to prognosis the trade turnover of Russia will increase furthermore with Asian countries, including China, Hong-Kong and Philippines in the next 15 years. Moreover, the imports from China will grow 11% annually. The main imported products will be electronically equipment whereas the share of telephone equipment will constitute 15.2%. (Vesti News Agency, 2012)

The demand for qualitative German machines and equipment is still high in Russia. The active participation of the Russian representatives in 2013 Hannover exhibition and presence of the Russian president Vladimir Putin there, shows the importance of bilateral trade relations between countries. According to the survey of Russian-German foreign trade committee in 2012, German companies plan to invest further 1 billion euro on business in Russia. Apart from 2014 Olympic Games in Sotschi, Formel 1 and World Football Championship will lead to huge state investments into infrastructure, construction of new buildings and agriculture. Only state owned railway company plans to invest 27 billion Euros. Vladimir Putin stated that in the framework of new projects it is expected creation of 25 million qualified work places in Russia. This economic progress in Russia opens new opportunities for exports German companies especially for those who are currently active in Russia. The recent entrance of Russia and periodical liberalization of the domestic market will gradually pave the way for German companies. (Exportmanager, 2013)

The success of German exports and overall trade relations periodically is affected by political processes. The current confrontation over Ukraine's political future and human rights issue in Russia has constrained the relations between countries. This fluctuation in the relations has concerned the business circles of Germany.

The head of "East Committee of German Economy" *(OA der Deutschen Wirtschaft)* Eckhard Cordes referring to the conducted survey of the committee stated that, 54% of questioned companies agreed that the relations between Germany and Russia have deteriorated. 44% of surveyed companies are in the opinion that Germany does not pay needed attention to Russia.

There are several requirements of German businessmen regarding Russia: removal of visa regime, establishment of free trade zones between EU and customs union of Russia, Belarus and Kazakhstan, improvement of infrastructure in the east Europe. The committee stressed the opportunities created due to world football championship in 2018, expansion of Moscow city, construction of new state building and also application of Yekaterinburg for hold of world expo 2020. (Russia Today news agency, 2013)

5   ANALYSIS OF THE THEORIES OF COMPETITION AND INNOVATION

5.1 Does the export competition between China and Germany contribute to innovation of their economies?

In the previous chapter, it was mentioned that according to Aghion, Howitt and other authors there is an inverted U relationship between competition and innovation. The opposite theory Schumpeterian model claims that the competition reduces the incentive as it limits the profit for certain company. Later Aghion and Howit (2001) have reconciled their theory with Schumpeterian model, that competition may fail the laggard companies who are far away from technical frontier. (Aghion et al, 2001, p. 2) The competition drives innovation in the neck and neck industries where the companies are able to catch up with each other. In this case the firms have similar production costs and their performance does not differ significantly. In contrast in less neck and neck and unbalanced industries the intensive competition may limit the profits of laggards and drive them out. If the level of competition is low then there is a possibility of escape of competition effect for less technologically developed firms. (Aghion et al, 2001, p. 3)

Innovation has already been one of the key indicators of competitiveness of nations. Moreover, it is the main driving engine of economic growth and technological progress that meet challenges of environment and health. The current global warming and other environmental problems have necessitated the innovation of technologies and transition to green technologies. (OECD, 2007, p. 3) In this regard not only western countries but also new emerging powers have performed quite well. BRIC countries have added value in their exports and achieved significant results in terms of innovation. (OECD, 2007, p. 8)

The role of China in world economy has grown enormously in the last decades and after entrance to WTO the trade pressure on European countries has further increased. The work of RCEP under London School of Economics has investigated the impact of growing Chinese exports on innovation and technological change in 12 countries of Europe including Germany.

The authors of research work have stated several key points regarding the impact of Chinese exports on European countries: strengthened technological

56

change within firms, redistributed employment towards more technologically developed firms, decrease in employment, profits, prices and the portion of low skilled worker. The competition pressure from China accounted for 15% upgrading of technologies in Europe between 2000 and 2007. (Bloom, Draca & Van Reenen, 2011, p. 2)

The research has yielded two main results: Firstly, Chinese export competition strengthens innovation, TFP and administration quality among surviving firms. The companies who are more affected by competition pressure of China tend to create more patents, increase expenditures on R&D, improve the efficiency of IT, employ more effective management methods and increase the TFP. Secondly, The Chinese competition drives out the technologically low advanced firms and reduce the employment level. Another interesting fact is that, the exports of low wage countries, including China have more positive effect on innovation rather than exports of high wage countries. This happens because Chinese exports make low-tech products not profitable anymore and it generates incentives to innovate and produce new goods. (Bloom, Draca & Van Reenen, 2011, p. 4)

Table 7 - Impact of Chinese exports on increase of patents per worker, IT and TFP in Europe

PANEL A: Increase in Patents per employee attributable to Chinese imports (as a % of the total increase over the period)				
Period	Within	Between	Exit	Total
2000-07	5.8	6.3	2.5	14.7

PANEL B: Increase in IT per employee attributable to Chinese imports (as a % of the total increase over the period)				
Period	Within	Between	Exit	Total
2000-07	9.8	3.1	1.2	14.1

PANEL C: Increase in Total Factor Productivity attributable to Chinese imports (as a % of the total increase over the period)				
Period	Within	Between	Exit	Total
2000-07	8.1	3.4	0.3	11.8

Source: RCEP under LSE (2011, p. 44)

From this table we can see that, in the period 2000-2007 Chinese export competition has accounted for 14.7% growth in patenting per worker, 14.1%

increase in IT intensity and 11.8% growth in TFP. The increase in patenting made up 13.9% in 2000-2004 and 18.7% in 2004-2007. The growth difference in periods occurred in accordance with increase of Chinese exports to Europe. (Bloom, Draca & Van Reenen, 2011, p.23)

The export competition pressure from China has also impact on skill upgrading in Europe. Mion and Linke Zhu (2010) have used the Belgian manufacturing firm-level date in the period 1996-2007 to research this issue. According to authors the imports from China decrease the employment growth but stimulate skill improvement. The reduction in employment growth is observed mainly in low tech firms. The impact of Chinese competition accounts for 42% within firm increase in the number of highly skilled workers in Belgium. (Mion and Linke Zhu, 2010, p. 2)

Figure 19 - The impact of Chinese competition on skill upgrading in Belgian companies

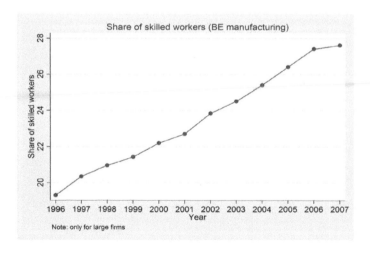

The impact of Chinese exports on Belgium market has both positive and negative sides. On the one hand it reduces the employment growth of low tech

companies and on the other hand it pushes firms to upgrade their skills in order to survive. (Mion and Linke Zhu, 2010, p.22)

Another point regarding the competition and innovation has focused on research and development (R&D). Gilbert has pointed to correlation between competition$\rightarrow$ R&D $\rightarrow$ innovation and stressed the importance of intellectual property rights. The inventor can fully enjoy its invention if there is a possibility to license and patent. (Gilbert, 2006, p. 5) Naturally the existence of intellectual property rights depends on the level of rule of law in the country, but in the international level the regulation of this issue is more complex. If look at the quality and effectiveness of public institutions both in Russia and China there is less probability that intellectual property rights are protected in high level. In regard to public institutions Russia takes 121 place and China 110th place according to GCI 2013/2014.

The situation in Germany differs significantly and the country ranked in 15th place. Unfortunately, China and Russia are among main actors who violate intensively the intellectual property rights. In 2005 at the German border there were confiscated goods in value of 215 million Euros and one third out of it came to share of China. The main reasons of piracy in China are considered to be violation of international agreements, the shortages in law implementation and limited freedom of media. (Schneider, 2008, p. 1) The piracy and imitation of products has a profound negative impact on innovation and overall performance of companies. On the one hand the turnover and market share of the firm decrease and on the other hand there is a necessity to combat piracy which requires high expenditures. (Schneider, 2008, p. 22)

5.2 ARE BOTH ECONOMIES ENOUGH COMPETITIVE IN ORDER TO CO-EXIST?

China has been the most successful exporter in the last few decades and in 2008 it became the biggest exporter in the world. The growing exports of China have caused concerns among EU member countries.

Periodically it is getting difficult for European countries to compete with China who exports relatively cheaper products. It is rare case that European countries have entered the market that is not yet conquered by China excepting

Germany. (Bekovskis & Silgoner, 2014, p. 1) According to findings of CompNet mainly small, CEE countries are exposed to tough competition pressure from China. (Bekovskis & Silgoner, 2013, p. 1) In spite of this fact there is not "cut-throat" competition between China and EU countries. (Bekovskis & Silgoner, 2013, p. 3)

The market share of China has increased from 4% up to 12% in the period 1999-2010. (Bekovskis & Silgoner, 2013, p. 2) This rapid growth of China has been main topic of researchers and in this regard the reaction of European countries especially Germany to this process is interesting. To what extent Germany has been able to withstand the competition pressure of China and has it been driven out from its market shares?

In the previous chapters we showed that China took leadership over Germany in Russian market. However, in most cases Germany has been successful in protecting its export shares and even in some cases it has entered the markets where Chinese firms have exited. In the period of 2000-2009 European, countries have been able to withstand the competition pressure of China, however this pressure is rising periodically. Eastern European countries are mostly exposed to competition from China and the possibilities to expand exports will be limited for them. Countries that are specialized on specific production where they are more competitive can avoid cut-throat competition of China. (Bekovskis & Silgoner, 2013, p. 4)

The impact of China on Europe is both positive and negative. On the one hand cheaper products of China increase the purchase ability of European consumers. The cheaper input products used for manufacture in Europe make them more competitive in the world markets. On the other hand China enters the export destinations of European countries and creates the threat of driving out. The level of competition between EU countries and China are similar. The figure below shows that the competition level between EU countries, including Germany and China has increased from 49% in 2001 up to 62% in 2009.

The overlap in markets with China is noticed in smaller and eastern European countries not in largest exporters like Germany. (Bekovskis & Silgoner, 2013, p. 5) The countries like Portugal, Sweden, Ireland, Denmark and Czech Republic are more exposed to competition pressure of China.

Figure 20 - Competition between China and European countries

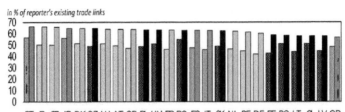

Source: UN COMTRADE, authors' calculations.   Shaded bars = 2001; solid bars = 2009.

Source: Bekovskis & Silgoner (2013, p. 27)

From the figure 20 it is clear that larger exporters of Europe including Germany have positioned themselves better against competition pressure of China. However, the increasing exports of China put growing pressure on all EU countries. The overall performance of EU member countries including Germany in world market and their crowding out are currently satisfactory. The best position belongs to Germany where the crowding out makes up 4.8% in compare of 10% in eastern European countries. The figure 21 shows the percentage of crowding out of EU member countries in the world competition. It is observed that the trend of driving out has grown from 2001 up to 2009. (Bekovskis & Silgoner, 2013, p. 30)

Figure 21 - Crowding out of EU countries in the world competition

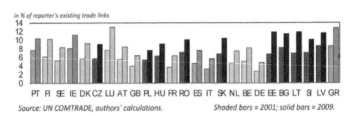

Source: UN COMTRADE, authors' calculations.   Shaded bars = 2001; solid bars = 2009.

Source: Bekovskis & Silgoner (2013, p. 29)

The figure 22 describes the crowding out of EU countries as a result of competition pressure from China. 80% of driving out cases of European countries from the market refers to China. There are also cases where larger exporters of Europe mainly Germany drives China from the market out. Competition pressure

61

of China as it was mentioned before hits small and peripheral countries of EU namely Belgium, Latvia, Lithuania, Greece, Portugal and Greece. The last three European countries in 90% of crowding out cases have left market because of Chinas entrance (Bekovskis & Silgoner, 2013, p. 30)

Figure 22 - Crowding out of EU countries by China

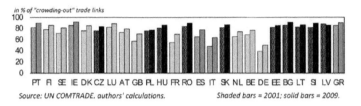

Source: Bekovskis & Silgoner (2013, p. 30)

It is obviously seen from the figure 22 that the crowding out of European countries has grown since 2001 and this trend continues. Germany is least affected and exposed to competition posed by China. According to analysis of Bekovskis and Silgoner (2013) the competition pressure from China is manageable and there is enough from for export destinations and products. With the growing global production chain the individual countries could specialize on specific areas of this production process. This is more necessary for smaller European countries that are more exposed to competition with China.

In order to be successful in exports the EU countries including Germany could strengthen existing trade relationships and discover new products and destinations for exports. The research has shown that in the last few decades European countries have been able to keep their existing trade relationships despite the growing Chinese competition. (Bekovskis & Silgoner, 2013, p. 32) The world demand for traded goods is not static and it fluctuates periodically. In this respect, Germany should be flexible in order to react to changing demand patterns. To keep the market even at hard times should be priority rather than leaving it and establishing new trade link. It is easier to revive after crisis than establishing new trade connections. (Bekovskis & Silgoner, 2014, p. 9)

5.3 IS CHINA A THREAT FOR GERMAN EXPORTS?

The economic relations between China and Germany are multidimensional. On the one hand the competition pressure from China rises and on the other hand China is becoming very important export destination for Germany. Moreover, the relocation of German companies to China enables them to keep competitiveness in the world markets and profit from opportunities offered in China. Both countries are export oriented and exports make up significant share of their economies.

Taking into consideration both positive and negative impact of China on Germany there emerges a question: Is China a threat for German exports or it enriches the economy of Germany? The survey conducted by TNS Infratest research institute in September-October of 2012 gives us to grasp some ideas regarding how China is perceived in Germany.

The inquiry of research institute includes 170 interviews among small, medium and bigger companies (economic decision makers), 1000 interviews among people over 18 years old (people), 80 interviews among politicians and the analysis of media in Germany (*Der Spiegel, Die Welt, Handelsblatt* and etc.). (Huawei Studies & Infratest research institute, 2012, p. 10/12) 88% of questioned

German citizens assume that China is very strong economic power and takes the first place or positions at least in the top 3 economic powers of the world. This opinion is supported by politicians and economic decision makers with 94-96%. The figure 23 shows the opinion of different social groups in Germany regarding the threat and enrichment role of China for German economy.

Figure 23 - Enrichment and threat role of China

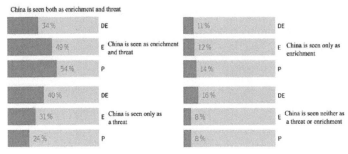

China is seen both as enrichment and threat

34%	DE	
49%	E	China is seen as enrichment and threat
54%	P	
40%	DE	
31%	E	China is seen only as a threat
24%	P	

11%	DE	
12%	E	China is seen only as enrichment
14%	P	
16%	DE	
8%	E	China is seen neither as a threat or enrichment
8%	P	

German people (DE) n=1000, Economic desicion makers (E) n=170, Politicians (P) n=80

Source: TNS Infratest (2012, p. 88)

The results of survey were also affected by knowledge of questioned individuals about China. The people who are in close contact with China or have business with this country expressed optimistic views regarding the impact on Germany. Another aspect that was researched by Infratest institute was the reasons why Germans perceive China as a threat.

As it is well known for many of us the price policy of China puts pressure not only on German exports but also on the exports of other countries. German companies perceive the price strategy of China as a threat for their performance and work places dependent on it. 71% of surveyed German people and economic decision makers agreed that cheaper prices of China pose a threat. The opinion of politicians regarding this issue is even higher reaching 74%. (Huawei Studies & Infratest research institute, 2012, p. 88)

Another aspect that makes German people to worry is that Chinese products drive out German products from the markets. However, this fear is less problematic and on average the half of surveyed people considers it as real threat. The reason of it could be the belief that lower quality Chinese products don't put much competition pressure on higher quality German products. (Huawei Studies & Infratest research institute, 2012, p. 90)

Figure 24 - Price policy and crowding out threat of China to Germany

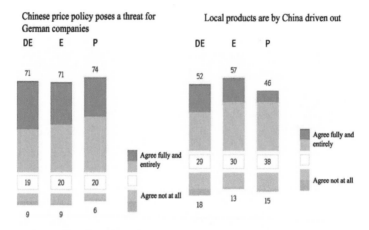

German people (DE) n=1000, Economic desicion makers (E) n=170, Politicians (P) n=80

Source: TNS Infratest (2012, p. 90)

China is developing rapidly also in the field of innovation. The opinion of surveyed individuals corresponds to this fact: 56% of German people placed china in the first place or in the top three positions, economic decision makers 43% and politicians 59%. The questioned groups unanimously supported the idea that China will grow furthermore as innovator. Actually China is in the fourth place after USA, Japan and Germany according to international applications for patents. If take into consideration that the main advantage of Germany is its innovative and qualitative products in the world market the growth of innovation power of China poses a competition pressure. (Huawei Studies & Infratest research institute, 2012, p. 93)

In the previous chapter it was mentioned that Russia imports mainly machinery and transport means from both China and Germany. It means that both countries are competing on the exports of these products on Russian market. The analysis shows that exactly these areas of German exports are under threat of Chinese competition.

Currently China is leader in the exports of machinery with 563 billion Euros and Germany takes fourth position with 230 billion Euros (2012). (Huawei Studies & Infratest research institute, 2012, p. 94)

Figure 25 - Threatened economic areas of Germany by competition pressure of China

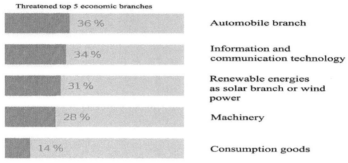

Threatened top 5 economic branches

36 %	Automobile branch
34 %	Information and communication technology
31 %	Renewable energies as solar branch or wind power
28 %	Machinery
14 %	Consumption goods

Basis: Economic deciosion makers n=170

Source: TNS Infratest, (2012, p. 94)

The automobile industry has been assessed as the most threatened area in spite of the fact that Germany is very competitive and successful on this area. For example the share of Volkswagen in China made up 19% in 2011.

According to German state statistics institution 308000 automobiles in value of 11.9 billion Euros were exported to China in 2011. It is 22.8% more than previous year. However periodically Chinese automobile industry catches up and acts as a rival for German automobiles in the world markets especially in developing countries. Another factor that provokes concerns in Germany is transfer of "know-how" and technology through Chinese investments and acquisitions in Germany. (28% of all Chinese investments in Germany make up machinery and automobile industry). (Huawei Studies & Infratest research institute, 2012, p. 94) 80-90% of all surveyed groups supported the idea that Chinese companies are copying western products and spying out new inventions and ideas. The figure 26 shows the opinion of surveyed people regarding this issue. (Huawei Studies & Infratest research institute, 2012, p. 96)

Figure 26 - Opinion of Germans regarding piracy stemming from China

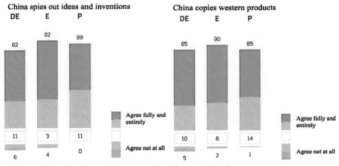

Source: TNS Infratest, (2012, p. 97)

The share of information and communication technologies in China has grown both in the domestic market and also in exports to foreign markets. Huawei technologies and Lenovo are among top 3 companies of the world in the sphere of information and communication technologies. China is leader in exports of data processing equipment and electronics to Germany with 35% share. The growing imports from China to Germany cause to concerns of local German producers. (Huawei Studies & Infratest research institute, 2012, p.95)

So far we discussed the threats posed to German exports by China, but there also positive impacts. Chinese investments in Germany create new job places. There are 900 Chinese companies functioning in Germany with 7300 employees. Huawei is the biggest Chinese company in Germany with 1600 worker. The lower productions costs enable China to export cheaper products and be competitive in the world markets. However, Germany also profits from this opportunity. Many German companies are relocating production facilities to China in order to benefit from lower production costs. 62% of surveyed economic decision makers replied that they have either facility or supplier in China.

83% of them estimate China as very important factor for their success. As it was mentioned before China is a very big export market for Germany and annual growth rate constitutes 20%. (Huawei Studies & Infratest research institute, 2012, p. 98)

6   MEETING CHALLENGES OF COMPETITION IN GLOBAL ECONOMY

So far the current competition between Germany and China was discussed. In order to protect sustainability of exports the global challenges should be met. The future of export competition will heavily depend on innovative capability of countries to produce green technologies and decrease the dependence on traditional energy resources. The natural resources in the world are limited and it necessitates countries to think over alternatives. It can also enable certain country to be competitive in the world markets and export successfully. Moreover, the protection of climate and environment is a top priority for both Germany and China. The health of ecology and environment currently does not end in the borders of any country but extends to the whole earth. The population of the world gradually grows and it challenges countries to take measure in order to meet demands of people.

Shell predicts that the demand for energy will be tripled by 2050 from 2000 levels. It is expected that China will consume 70% more energy than the USA by 2035.Today around 50% of energy generation comes from renewable energy sources. It is estimated that by 2050 77% of world energy demand could be met by renewable energy sources. Together with it, it is expected that the energy generation of nuclear power plants will grow 70% by 2035. The number of passenger cars will reach around 1.7 billion units by 2035 doubling the current quantity. It raises concerns both about fuelling so many cars and its negative impact on environment. (Millennium project, 2012)

In order to keep sustainability of German and Chinese exports the transfer into green technologies are very important. China is emitting more CO_2 emissions than developed countries and exported products are main reason of pollution.

On the one hand China has encountered with environmental problems and faces world pressure to reduce carbon emissions. On the other hand it is short of natural resources and depends on imports. To tackle this global challenge China has prepared strategies and policies in order to transfer to conservation oriented society and developing green technology. (BCAS Chinese academy of sciences, 2012, p. 4)

According to recent Bloomberg report China spent 49billion US dollars on renewable energies in 2010. It is 28% more than previous year. It accounted for almost ¼ of global investment $211 billion. In the same period Germany took second place with $41 Billion 100% more than previous year. The development of solar and wind energy in China puts also competition pressure on Germany. It is hard to say if competition or cooperation on this sphere is more rational in order to achieve the common goal of protecting the environment. The recycling is another very important aspect of sustainability. Germany recycles 70% of used paper that is higher than the average 56% in the EU. The country also performs well in recycling 90% of used glass. (Deutsche Welle, 2011)

The sustainability of export led growth of China has also caused discussions among economic experts. There are sceptics and also supporters of the idea that China will grow furthermore and be the largest economy of the world. Guo and N'Diaye (2009) have researched this issue and have concluded that in order to keep sustainability of export led growth China will have to take certain measures. China will need fast increase exports and major shares in the world markets. It is a big challenge for China because the global demand and global economy grows slowly.

In order to get significant market shares China will have to reduce prices especially for its key industries like steel, shipbuilding and machine tools. The reduction of prices could be accomplished through combination of these measures 1) Strengthening productivity with lower costs in compare of competitors 2) Decrease in corporate profits 3) Subsidies through price distortions. (Guo & N'Diaye, 2009, p. 3) However, it is possible that all these measures might be not enough for export expansion in the near future. Expanding value added chain, accessing new industries, diversifying exports, increasing domestic value added of exports and expanding globalization could enable further expansion of exports.

The experience of Asian countries like Japan and Korea who had similar export lead growth suggests that these might be not enough to expand market shares. Strengthening domestic consumption through structural reforms that reduce precautionary savings could impact positively on output growth and decrease the need for acquiring new market shares.

69

It can prevent China from heavily depending on overseas export that had negative impacts on Japanese and Korean economy. (Guo & N'Diaye, 2009, p. 4)

It is expected that the economic growth of Germany could slow down 1% in the coming decades if structural reforms would not be taken. The employment rate might decrease ½ percent in the period between 2016 and 2025 as the German population ages. The slowdown in the economic growth will negatively affect GDP per capita as the working age population decreases faster than the total population. It is estimated that the number of people aged under 15 and above 64 relative to working age population will increase from 51% now up to 74% by the mid 2030s. (OECD, 2012, p. 11)

In order to foster the economic growth the reforms and appropriate policies should be realized. In terms of full female employment Germany lags behind among OECD countries. The working hours of females in Germany amount to 30.5 hours which is 10 hours fewer than male working hours. Increasing work hours for females might reduce income gap between male and females and also contribute to the growth of labour input. Another factor that hinders labour productivity is tough regulations regarding social benefits. For example free health insurance for unemployed spouse or joint taxation of spouses overall income. (OECD, 2012, p. 12)

Prolonging longer work life could be another contribution for increasing labour input. The reforms of 2000s that limited early retirement option Germany managed to reach 57% employment of people aged 57% in 2010. It is higher than OECD average but could also be raised up to 70% that exists in Sweden, Norway and New Zealand. Fostering integration and labour migration is necessary reform that could solve some problems in the labour market. (OECD, 2012, p. 13)

Immigration of workers to Germany accounts for small portion of overall immigration. Especially the share of educated immigrants is small in compare of other OECD countries. It is reasonable that the access of non EU citizens with high skills is eased in order to enter labour market of Germany. It is also not easy for employer to hire a non EU citizen as the requirements are not flexible. First of all the employer should prove that there are not employees that could fill the position and moreover the income of hired non EU citizen should exceed 66000

Euros. The flexibility in such regulations could foster the immigration of highly skilled workers to Germany. (OECD, 2012, p. 15)

The future of energy sector will heavily depend of renewable energy sources (RES). Currently the price of energy generation through RES is not cheaper relatively to fossil based energy generation. Increasing competition on this sector could lead to reduction of prices. Moreover the entrance of foreign competitors should be ensured. Eco innovation is very important not only for fighting climate change but also for economic growth. Currently Germany performs well on this sphere and it was second after Japan for patent application in the period between 1996 and 2008. (OECD, 2012, p. 22)

7   CONCLUSION

The thesis has researched the impact of competition on innovation and growth of Chinese and German economies. Several contradictory theories have been applied to research different aspects of export competition between countries. Aghion (2002) has reconciled his theory - an inverted U relationship between competition and innovation - with Schumpeterian concept allowing technologically advanced enterprises to innovate. There are few chances for laggard firms to survive the tough competition. In contrast technologically developed companies respond to competition pressure with innovation and escape competition effect.

The theory of Aghion and his co-authors (2002) have been supported via research of "Centre for Economic Performance" under LSE. The research has revealed that China accounted for 15% of technological upgrading in Europe between 2000 and 2007. The companies who face more competition pressure put much effort to create more patents, raise investment on R&D, improve IT intensity, apply effective management methods and increase the TFP.

In the period between 2000 and 2007 Chinese competition pressure has accounted for 14.7% increase in patenting per worker, 14.1% in IT intensity and 11.8% in TFP. The European companies improve their skill capabilities in order to resist Chinese competition.

71

In this regard the case of Belgium firms has been applied to explain the process. The number of skilled workers within companies has increased 42% in the period between 1996 and 2007 as a result of competition from China. Chinese companies drive out mainly technologically poor equipped firms that cannot withstand competition pressure. Ousted firms also cause to reduction in employment rate.

The export competition of Germany and China in Russian market is very intensive. China has already passed Germany as a main exporter in Russian market. The trade turnover between countries is expected to reach 100 billion US dollar by 2015. The success of countries in Russian market is heavily affected by ongoing political processes. The recent conflict over the future destiny of Ukraine strained the relations between Germany and Russia which caused to concerns of German companies operating in Russia. Despite the political factor the German products are competitive in Russian market in terms of their high quality. However, periodically Chinese exports represent the mixture of quality and price – a strategy that really challenges German exports.

The importance of intellectual property protection has been focus of many researches and studies. There is a correlation between innovation and intellectual property protection. An inventor needs assurance that he will be able to enjoy the new invention and profit from it. Unfortunately, there is a negative impact of China on innovation in Germany in terms of protection of intellectual property.

In 2005 there were confiscated fake goods in value of 215 million Euros in German border and 1/3 of it came from China. The main reasons of piracy in China are weak rule of law, limited freedom of media and violation of international agreements. The copy and imitation of products in China destroys the incentives for innovation and decreases the profit of innovative companies.

"Competitiveness Research Network" has concluded that Germany is the least exposed to competition pressure from China. Moreover, German companies are not being crowded out by Chinese firms in the world markets. The competition pressure from China also causes to skill upgrading in Europe, including in Germany in order to keep competitiveness. The results of research give clearly to understand that both countries are highly competitive in order to be successful in the world exports. However, it is recommended that both countries increase the domestic demand in order not to overfish in the same pool.

The opinion of different social groups in Germany is different in regard to growing economic power of China. The majority of Germans perceive China as a threat rather than enrichment for economy. Surveyed economic decision-makers, politicians and ordinary people think that Chinese products drive out German goods from world markets. This concern is not threatening because the people also consider Chinese products of low quality. The questioned individuals consider China as an innovative nation and assume that in the future the innovative capability of the country will further increase. Mostly threatened German industries are considered to be automobile branch, ICT, renewable energies and machinery.

German businessmen have also expressed positive ideas about China especially those who are in close touch with China. 62% of surveyed business people have either facility or supplier in China. They have estimated China as a very important factor for their success.

The future perspectives of German and Chinese exports will be directly connected to transfer into green technologies and renewable energies. It is important not only to increase the profit but also to protect deteriorating world environment. Moreover, both countries could take appropriate measures in order to improve competitiveness in the world markets.

BIBLIOGRAPHY

1. Aghion et al, 2002, "competition and innovation: an inverted U relationship", Working Paper 9269

2. Aghion/Bessonova, 2006, "on entry and growth: theory and evidence"

3. Alterna International Trade Company", 2014, "Deliveries from China rise constantly", available on http://goo.gl/AJ5tPW

4. Pakhomov/ von Cramon-Taubadel 2013, "Architecture and dynamics of Russian-German economic relations"

5. Moshes/ Nojonen, 2011, "Russia-China relations: The Current state, alternative futures, and implications for the West", Report

6. Panagariya, 2003, "China's Export Strategy: What Can We Learn From It?", working paper

7. Silburt, 2012, "Financing Obstacles for SMEs in China"

8. Avtostat analytical auto agency, 2012, "Import of Chinese automobiles to Russia can increase", available on http://goo.gl/oNCtWd

9. CBC special machines company, 2006, "China in automobile industry of Russia", available on http://goo.gl/Ax9uWo

10. CIA world factbook China, 2014, available on http://goo.gl/WfVrE

11. Onori, 2013, "Competition and growth: reinterpreting their relationship", WP 2013 - Nr 24

12. *Der Spiegel, Die Welt, Handelsblatt* and etc.. Huawei Studies/Infratest research institute, 2012, "Germany and China - perception and reality"

13. Destatis, 2011, "Export, import and globalization"

14. Destatis, 2013, GDP of Germany, available on http://goo.gl/SoVwkF

15. Deutsche Welle, 2011, "China and Germany seize lead in green technologies", http://goo.gl/Cmcrpp

16. *Deutsch-Russische AH*, 2014, Pressemeldung

17. *Deutsch-Russische AHK/OA der Deutschen Wirtschaft, 2013, Geschäftsklima in Russland,* survey

18. DIHK 2012, „*Markt, Modernisierung, Mittelstand*", annual report

19. DIHK, 2011, „*Russland nach der parlamentswahl und vor dem WTO-Beitritt*"

20. DIHK, 2011/2012, *"Der Deutsche Aussenhandel*"

21. Yalchin/ Zacher, 2011, *"Zur Lage der deutschen Exporte"*

74

22. Exportmanager- publication of F.A.Z institute, 2013, "Russia's modernization is based on German technology", available on http://goo.gl/OFI1px

23. Adams et al, 2004, "Why is China so competitive?", working paper № 04-6

24. Federal ministry for economic affairs and energy of Germany, 2013, "German *Mittelstand*: Engine of the German economy"

25. Federal Ministry of Economics and Energy, 2012, "annual economic report - boosting confidence"

26. Federal Ministry of Economics and Technology, 2013, "2013 annual economic report"

27. Federal Ministry of Education and Research, 2007, "ICT 2020 – research for innovations"

28. Mion & Linke Zhu, 2010, Import Competition from and Outsourcing to China: A Curse or Blessing for Firms?", discussion paper № 1038

29. Global Competitiveness Report 2013/2014

30. GTA, AHK, Embassy of Germany in Moscow, 2013, *"Russland in Zahlen"*, Report

31. GTAI, 2011, "infrastruktur", available on http://goo.gl/mqPbw

32. GTAI, 2013, "Economic Overview Germany: Market, productivity, innovation

33. Huawei Studies & Infratest research institute, 2012, "Germany and China - perception and reality", survey

34. IMF, available on http://goo.gl/rFHDww

35. Internet Portal of Foreign Trade, MEDR, available on http://goo.gl/QXt23j

36. Alexandrovich, 2012, "Dynamics and structure of Russian-Chinese Trade", research analysis

37. Harrigan & Deng, 2010, "China's Local Comparative Advantage"

38. Guo & N'Diaye, 2009, "Is China's Export-Oriented Growth Sustainable?", IMF working paper WP/09/172

39. Librondt, 2013, "Economization of German security policy. The case of German-Russian relations". Working paper

40. Bekovskis & Silgoner, 2013, "Crowding out or co-existence? The competitive position of EU and China in Global Merchandise trade", CompNet policy brief № 1617

41. Bekovskis et al, 2014, "Mapping competitive pressure between China and EU countries", CompNet policy brief № 4

42. Li & Fung research centre, 2012, „An Update on the Transport Infrastructure Development in China"

43. MEDR, Internet Portal of Foreign Economic relations of Russia, available on http://goo.gl/CJROl9

44. Millennium project, 2012, "Global challenges facing humanity", available on http://goo.gl/9KekCL

45. Bloom, Draca and Van Reenen, 2011, "Trade induced technical change? The impact of Chinese imports on innovation, IT and productivity", discussion paper № 1000

46. Godfrey, 2008, "Why is competition important for growth and poverty reduction?", work paper *OA der Deutschen Wirtschaft*

47. OECD better life index, available on http://goo.gl/EcLNHy

48. OECD economic survey Germany,.2012,

49. OECD employment outlook, 2013, "how does Germany compare",

50. OECD, 2007, "Innovation and growth rationale for an innovation strategy"

51. OECD, 2012, "Science, technology and industry outlook"

52. OECD, 2011, "Education at a glance – China"

53. OECD, 2012, "China in focus. Lessons and challenges"

54. Policonomics economic dictionary, available on http://goo.gl/6yQjRP

55. Reem Hekal 2009, "What are economies of scale", 2009, available on http://goo.gl/sfNhZr

56. Gilbert, 2006, "Looking for Mr. Schumpeter: Where Are We in the Competition Innovation Debate?"

57. D. Atkinson, 2013, "Competitiveness, Innovation and Productivity: Clearing up the confusion", report

58. Russia Today News Website, 2013, "Putin seeks to boost trade with China to new record $100bln", available on http://goo.gl/0Ue9Hy

59. Starsenal construction machinery company of Russia, "Promotion of Chinese construction machinery in Russian market", available on http://goo.gl/lBU45e

60. Danninger & Joutz, 2007, "What Explains Germany's Rebounding Export Market Share?", IMF working paper WP/07/24

61. Bell & Chao, 2010, "The financial system in China: risks and opportunities following the financial crisis", White Paper.

62. V. Lawrence, 2013, "Understanding China's Political System", Report for congress

63. Palley, 2011, "The Rise and Fall of Export-led Growth", working paper № 675

64. Trade and economic office of Russian embassy in Berlin, 2013, "Trade turnover between Germany and Russia for January-September 2013", Report

65. Transparency International, available on http://goo.gl/nbp55B

66. Vesti News Agency, 2012, "The most attractive partners of Russia in the next 15 years", available on http://goo.gl/QgtY3X

67. VW, available on http://goo.gl/JzNKlL

68. wordpress, 2012, "Trends in China's labour market" available on http://goo.gl/g6o2PX

69. Xinhua News Agency, 2013, "Russia welcomes more Chinese investment in Russian Far East: Medvedev", available on http://goo.gl/Dqin8P

70. Gorodnichenko et al, 2008, "Globalization and innovation in emerging markets", Working Paper 14481